# Voltaire's Candide: A Discussion Guide

David Bruce

Published by David Bruce, 2022.

VOLTAIRE'S CANDIDE: A DISCUSSION GUIDE

**First edition. October 30, 2022.**



ISBN: 979-8215500835

Written by David Bruce.

# Table of Contents

# Dedication

**Dedicated to Carl Eugene Bruce and Josephine Saturday Bruce**

My father, Carl Eugene Bruce, died on 24 October 2013. He used to work for Ohio Power, and at one time, his job was to shut off the electricity of people who had not paid their bills. He sometimes would find a home with an impoverished mother and some children. Instead of shutting off their electricity, he would tell the mother that she needed to pay her bill or soon her electricity would be shut off. He would write on a form that no one was home when he stopped by because if no one was home he did not have to shut off their electricity.

The best good deed that anyone ever did for my father occurred after a storm that knocked down many power lines. He and other linemen worked long hours and got wet and cold. Their feet were freezing because water got into their boots and soaked their socks. Fortunately, a kind woman gave my father and the other linemen dry socks to wear.

My mother, Josephine Saturday Bruce, died on 14 June 2003. She used to work at a store that sold clothing. One day, an impoverished mother with a baby clothed in rags walked into the store and started shoplifting in an interesting way: The mother took the rags off her baby and dressed the infant in new clothing. My mother knew that this mother could not afford to buy the clothing, but she helped the mother dress her baby and then she watched as the mother walked out of the store without paying.

***

The doing of good deeds is important. As a free person, you can choose to live your life as a good person or as a bad person. To be a good person, do good deeds. To be a bad person, do bad deeds. If you do good deeds, you will become good. If you do bad deeds, you will become bad. To become the person you want to be, act as if you already are that kind of person. Each of us chooses what kind of person we will become. To become a good person, do the things a good person does. To become a bad person, do the things a bad person does. The opportunity to take action to become the kind of person you want to be is yours.

Human beings have free will. According to the Babylonian Niddah 16b, whenever a baby is to be conceived, the Lailah (angel in charge of contraception) takes the drop of semen that will result in the conception and asks God, "Sovereign of the Universe, what is going to be the fate of this drop? Will it develop into a robust or into a weak person? An intelligent or a stupid person? A wealthy or a poor person?" The Lailah asks all these questions, but it does not ask, "Will it develop into a righteous or a wicked person?" The answer to that question lies in the decisions to be freely made by the human being that is the result of the conception.

A Buddhist monk visiting a class wrote this on the chalkboard: "EVERYONE WANTS TO SAVE THE WORLD, BUT NO ONE WANTS TO HELP MOM DO THE DISHES." The students laughed, but the monk then said, "Statistically, it's highly unlikely that any of you will ever have the opportunity to run into a burning orphanage and rescue an infant. But, in the smallest gesture of kindness — a warm smile, holding the door for the person behind you, shoveling the driveway of the elderly person next door — you have committed an act of immeasurable profundity, because to each of us, our life is our universe."

In her book titled *I Have Chosen to Stay and Fight*, comedian Margaret Cho writes, "I believe that we get complimentary snack-size portions of the afterlife, and we all receive them in a different way." For Ms. Cho, many of her snack-size portions of the afterlife come in hip hop music. Other people get different snack-size portions of the afterlife, and we all must be on the lookout for them when they come our way. And perhaps doing good deeds and experiencing good deeds are snack-size portions of the afterlife.

Cover Photograph for Voltaire's *Candide*: A Discussion Guide: Erik Lucatero

https://pixabay.com/photos/portrait-people-adult-man-face-3353699/

# Preface

The purpose of this book is educational. I have read, studied, and taught Voltaire's *Candide*, and I wish to pass on what I have learned to other people who are interested in studying Voltaire's *Candide*.

This book uses a question-and-answer format. It poses, then answers, relevant questions about Voltaire, background information, and *Candide*. I recommend that you read the relevant section of *Candide*, then read my comments, then go back and re-read the relevant section of *Candide*. However, do what works for you.

Teachers may find this book useful as a discussion guide for the novel. Teachers can have students read chapters from this short novel, then teachers can ask students selected questions from this study guide.

This Discussion Guide does contain a certain amount of repetition. Repetition can be a useful teaching tool. Of course, in the classroom, teachers can skip the repetition that they don't think is useful. Also, many of the questions can be used for Short Reaction Memos. See Appendix E.

The long quotations from Voltaire's *Candide* in this study guide, unless otherwise indicated, come from an 18th-century translation by Tobias Smollett. The short quotations (with page numbers in parentheses) are from the translation by Lowell Bair (Bantam Classics edition).

This study guide will occasionally use short quotations from books about Voltaire and *Candide*. The use of these short quotations is consistent with fair use:

§ 107. Limitations on exclusive rights: Fair use

Release date: 2004-04-30

Notwithstanding the provisions of sections 106 and 106A, the fair use of a copyrighted work, including such use by reproduction in copies or phonorecords or by any other means specified by that section, for purposes such as criticism, comment, news reporting, teaching (including multiple copies for classroom use), scholarship, or research, is not an infringement of copyright. In determining whether the use made of a work in any particular case is a fair use the factors to be considered shall include

(1) the purpose and character of the use, including whether such use is of a commercial nature or is for nonprofit educational purposes;

(2) the nature of the copyrighted work;

(3) the amount and substantiality of the portion used in relation to the copyrighted work as a whole; and

(4) the effect of the use upon the potential market for or value of the copyrighted work.

The fact that a work is unpublished shall not itself bar a finding of fair use if such finding is made upon consideration of all the above factors.

Source of Fair Use information:

<http://www.law.cornell.edu/uscode/text/17/107>.

# "An Appreciation" (From the Bantam Edition)

**What are some anecdotes André Maurois tells about Voltaire? Can you find some other anecdotes about Voltaire?**

*Anecdotes by André Maurois*

• At Ferney, Voltaire played a daily game of chess with Father Adam, a Jesuit. One hopes that the father was a patient man, for when Voltaire was losing, he would overturn the board, playing the game to the end only when he was winning. (Source: Andre Maurois, "An Appreciation," Introduction to Voltaire, *Candide*, p. 2.)

• Voltaire was controversial and thought to be impious. Because of the attacks against him, he lived at Ferney, close to the border with Switzerland, where he could escape if necessary. While on her deathbed, Queen Maria Lecszinska wanted his impiety to be punished. However, her husband the King answered, "What can I do? If he were in Paris, I should exile him to Ferney." (Source: Andre Maurois, "An Appreciation," Introduction to Voltaire, *Candide*, p. 11.)

• During his life, Voltaire was often under attack by censors, and he lived close to the border so he could escape to Switzerland if necessary. When the case against Voltaire's *Man With Forty Crowns* was called, a magistrate asked, "Is it only his books we shall burn?" (Source: Andre Maurois, "An Appreciation," Introduction to Voltaire, *Candide*, pp. 11-12.)

• At Ferney, Voltaire had a church built. In it, he had a stage built for the performances of plays, saying, "If you meet any of the devout, tell them that I've built a church; if you meet pleasant people, tell them I've finished a theater." (Source: Andre Maurois, "An Appreciation," Introduction to Voltaire, *Candide*, pp. 2-3.)

• At Ferney, Voltaire had a church built. This inscription appeared over its porch: *Dei Erexit Voltaire*. Translated: "Voltaire Erected [This] to God." Visitors used to look at the inscription and remark, "Two great names." (Source: Andre Maurois, "An Appreciation," Introduction to Voltaire, *Candide*, p. 2.)

• At Ferney, Voltaire had a church built. He also had a tomb for himself built, half in and half out of the church. That way, Voltaire explained, "The rascals will say that I'm neither in nor out." (Source: Andre Maurois, "An Appreciation," Introduction to Voltaire, *Candide*, p. 2.)

*An Additional Anecdote*

• A man who wanted to start a new religion approached Voltaire for advice. Voltaire told him, "I would advise that you first get yourself crucified, then rise on the third day." (Source: John Deedy, *A Book of Catholic Anecdotes*, p. 243.)

**If you feel like doing research, give information about Voltaire's biography. (Avoid plagiarism — don't simply download information; instead, put the information in your own words and tell the source(s) of information you used.)**

• Voltaire lived from 1694 to 1778. He was a French writer who is today known primarily as a satirist. He crusaded against evil and ignorance, and he is an icon of the 18th-century Enlightenment. Today, Voltaire is primarily known for his satire *Candide*, which he published in 1759.

• The Enlightenment supported reason, science, and the equality of man. It influenced the American Revolution.

• Voltaire's full name was François-Marie Arouet (the name "Voltaire" was a pseudonym), and he was born on November 21, 1694 in Paris, France. King Louis XIV ruled France. The Jesuits have been known for providing excellent educations to many people, and the Jesuits educated Voltaire at the Collège Louis-le-Grand, which he attended from 1704 to 1711.

- Voltaire studied law from 1711 to 1713, and he worked as a secretary to the French ambassador serving in Holland, then a place of relative tolerance and freedom.

- Voltaire's satire and criticism frequently got him in trouble, including time spent in prison and time spent in exile. He criticized both the government and the Catholic Church, so he made many enemies. He hated tyranny and religious intolerance.

- For five months in 1716, Voltaire was forced into exile from Paris. He was imprisoned in the Bastille, a famous prison in Paris, from 1717 to 1718.

- In 1718, at age twenty-four, Voltaire wrote his first play, a tragedy titled *Oedipe*, which gained him fame.

- Voltaire became wealthy in 1726. He also again spent time in the Bastille in 1726. He was allowed to leave the Bastille as long as he moved to England.

- Voltaire stayed mainly in England, then relatively a place of tolerance and freedom, from 1726 to 1729. He was famous, and English VIPs loved him. He was also good at learning new languages, and he became fluent in English.

- Voltaire wrote much, often in English. Two essays that he wrote in English were "Essay Upon Epic Poetry" and "Essay Upon the Civil Wars in France," both of which were published in 1727.

- After three years in England, and back in France, Voltaire wrote his *Philosophical Letters*, a comparison of two governments: the English government and the French government. He preferred the English government, and so his book was banned and he had to go into exile from Paris again.

- Voltaire was elected to the French Academy in 1746.

- Voltaire spent time in Holland and in Berlin.

- In 1759, Voltaire bought an estate at Ferney, which was close to Switzerland. That way, if he needed to leave quickly, he could go to Switzerland, where he would be safe.

- In 1759, Voltaire published *Candide*, his most enduring work. Many historical events influenced his writing of his masterpiece:

  - In 1755, an earthquake hit Lisbon, Portugal, killing 30,000 to 40,000 people there. More people died in Morocco.

  - In 1756, the Seven Years' War began in the German states.

  - In 1757, the English Admiral John Byng was unjustly executed.

- On his return to Paris in February 1778, Voltaire was treated as a hero.
  - On May 30, 1778, at age 84, Voltaire died in Paris.

# Chapter 1: "How Candide was brought up in a beautiful castle, and how he was driven from it."

**Voltaire is an Enlightenment writer. What is the Enlightenment?**

• The Enlightenment is also known as the neoclassic movement. It followed and was influenced by the Renaissance, and it was both an artistic and a philosophical movement.

• The Enlightenment was an optimistic movement. It believed that Humankind can make progress in solving the problems of the world. By using reason and logic, Humankind can make things better. The Enlightenment supported reform of social structures.

• The Enlightenment was anti-ignorance. It supported science, and it rejected superstition.

• The Enlightenment loved Greco-Roman art, including literature and architecture.

• Enlightenment gardens were laid out in geometric patterns, reflecting the Enlightenment's love of geometry and mathematics.

• Enlightenment poets such as Alexander Pope and John Dryden used metrical patterns that were almost clocklike in their regularity (but they were masters at varying the rhythms for artistic effects).

• Enlightenment authors used satire. By criticizing society's evils, they were hoping to make society better. Voltaire's *Candide* attacks bad ideas and hopes to make society better.

• Dr. L. Kip Wheeler of Carson-Newman College in Jefferson City, Tennessee, writes this:

> For me, I have found one useful exercise to understand the difference between the Enlightenment and the Romantic aesthetic that followed. This exercise is examining the architecture of English and continental gardens in each

period. In the Enlightenment, the garden would be kept neatly trimmed, with only useful or decorative plants allowed to grow, and every weed meticulously uprooted. The trees would be planted according to mathematical models for harmonious spacing, and the shrubbery would be pruned into geometric shapes such as spheres, cones, or pyramids. The preferred garden walls would involve Greco-Roman columns perfectly spaced from each other in clean white marble, smoothly burnished in straight edges and lines. If a stream or well were available, the architect might divert it down a carefully designed irrigation path, or pump it into the spray of a marble fountain. Such a setting was considered ideal for hosting civilized gatherings and leisurely strolls through the grounds. Such features were common in gardens from the 1660s up through the late 1790s. Nature was something to be shaped according to the dictates of human will and tamed according to the rules of human logic.

On the other hand, the later Romanticists might be horrified at the artificial design imposed upon nature. The ideal garden in the Romantic period might be planted in the ruins of an ancient cloister or churchyard. Wild ivy might be encouraged to grow along the picturesque, rough-hewn walls. Rather than ornamental shrubbery, fruit trees would be planted. The flowers might be loosely clustered according to type, but overgrown random patterns caused by the natural distribution of wind and rain were considered more aesthetically pleasing. Even better, rather than planting a garden, a Romanticist nature-lover would be encouraged to [go] walking in the untamed wilderness, clambering up and down the uneven rocks and gullies of a natural stream. Many

Romanticists who inherited Enlightenment gardens simply tore the structures down and allowed the grounds to run wild. Nature was considered something larger than humanity, and the passions it inspired in its untamed form were considered healthier (more "natural") than the faint-hearted passions originating in falsely imposed human design.

Source: http://guweb2.gonzaga.edu/faculty/wheeler/lit_terms_E.html

Date: 25 June 2004

***Candide* can be regarded as a picaresque novel. What is a picaresque novel?**
• A picaresque novel has a vagabond, usually of low birth, as a hero. The vagabond wanders from place to place and has many adventures. In a picaresque novel, odd events occur, such as a character who is thought to be dead suddenly turning up very much alive. This happens often in *Candide*, which takes the picaresque novel to an extreme — it is a satire, after all.
• Picaresque novels often depict a corrupt society, which is certainly the case in *Candide*. Its hero lives by his wits, which is kind of the case in *Candide*, but the title character is naïve and frequently taken advantage of.

**Candide is a satire. Define "satire."**
• Satire is humorous criticism. The humor, however, can be scathing.
• Satire is an attempt to make the world better. By attacking and exposing human stupidity, the satirist hopes that the end result is that human stupidity is replaced with human intelligence.
• Satire was a popular literary device of the Enlightenment.

• Unfortunately, satire does not always work. Sometimes, people think that the satire is about someone else, not themselves.

• "Satire is a mirror in which people see everyone else's face but their own." — Jonathan Swift, author of "A Modest Proposal" and *Gulliver's Travels.*

**What do we learn about Candide and Cunegonde in Chapter 1?**

• Candide has a gentle character. He is described as having "rather sound judgment with great simplicity of mind" (17).

• Apparently, Candide is a bastard. According to the servants, Candide may be the love child of the Baron's sister, who would not marry the father because he could prove only 71 generations of nobility, while she herself has 72. (Exaggeration is an important part of satire.)

• Cunegonde is 17, plumb, and pretty.

• Candide thinks that Cunegonde is beautiful. She also has a romantic interest in Candide.

• Candide and Cunegonde are on the verge of having sex when they are discovered by the Baron, who drives Candide from his castle with kicks to the butt.

**Describe Pangloss' philosophy.**

• Pangloss believes that this is the "best of all possible worlds" (18).

• The Baron's castle is the best of all possible castles, and the baroness is the best of all possible baronesses.

• This philosophy seems rather silly. Certainly, it runs afoul against the existence of evil. Wouldn't the best of all possible worlds lack evil?

• Pangloss teaches "metaphysico-theologo-cosmonigology" (18). This word combines three fields of philosophy:

Metaphysics is the study of "being" or existence.
Theology is the study of God.
Cosmology is the study of the universe.

We also see the letters "nig" here. "Niggardly" meant "very little." We will see that Pangloss has very little intelligence, despite his education.

**If you feel like doing research, describe Gottfried Wilhelm von Leibniz (sometimes spelled Leibnitz) and philosophical optimism. (Avoid plagiarism.)**

• Gottfried Wilhelm von Leibniz (1646-1716), a mathematician, scientist, and philosopher, really did believe that this is the best of all possible worlds. He believed that partly on religious grounds. If God created the world, and if God is all-good, all-knowing, and all-powerful, then the world that He created must be the best of all possible worlds. Leibnitz' philosophy is that of philosophical optimism.

• Leibniz wrote his *Theodicy* (1710), in which he defended God against evil. A theodicy is a defense of God's divine attributes — all-good (omnibenevolent), all-knowing (omniscient), and all-powerful (omnipotent) — despite the presence of evil in the world.

• Evil exists, obviously, in this world, but Leibniz believed that this so-called evil must serve a higher purpose of which we are unaware.

• Voltaire will have none of this. Leibniz' philosophy was simplified by other people, and Voltaire attacks this simplified form. For example, poet Alexander Pope wrote, "What is, is right."

• Apparently, Voltaire believes that evil is evil, and that God could have designed a better world. To Voltaire, philosophical optimism leads to quietism — to do-nothingism. After all, if this already is the best of all possible worlds, then why try to change it to make it better?

• Possibly, Leibniz could be correct. Perhaps this world is not meant to keep us all safe and comfy, the way that we treat our pets. Perhaps this world is designed for another purpose.

• Theologian John Hick believes that this world is designed for the purpose of creating souls. We have free will, and we can develop our souls through using our free will. We can choose to be good people or bad people. In addition, our world is designed to obey the laws of nature/physics. Sometimes, natural evil can occur, and our responses to natural evil can also develop our souls.

• Voltaire may approve of these ideas. Evil exists, and we can develop our souls by fighting against evil. These ideas do not lead to quietism. Voltaire believes in reform and in fighting against evil.

• We see satire in Chapter 1 (and in all the other chapters of *Candide*). Voltaire is making fun of a particular kind of philosophy: philosophical optimism. Therefore, Voltaire makes use of philosophical terms in this chapter. Sex is described in terms of "cause and effect" (19) and in terms of "repeated experiments" (18). Pangloss has a "sufficient reason" (19-20) for having sex with a "chambermaid, a very pretty and docile little brunette" (18).

• Another thing we see in Chapter 1 is something that we will see over and over in *Candide*. A situation that seems very good suddenly becomes very bad. Candide and Cunegonde kiss, and suddenly Candide is thrown out of the castle. This, of course, happens "in this best of all possible worlds" (18).

• Very often in *Candide* we will see that the characters say one thing, but what is happening around them points to the opposite thing. We must be alert to recognize this when this happens.

**Which lesson in "experimental physics" (18) does Pangloss give the maid and Cunegonde wishes Candide to give to her?**

• Pangloss has sex with the agreeable maid, and Cunegonde wishes to have sex with Candide.

• Voltaire uses philosophical language here. Pangloss has a "sufficient reason" to have sex with the maid. That sufficient reason, of course, is a willing maid and a strong libido.

• Leibniz originated the term "sufficient reason." We can define the Principle of Sufficient Reason as saying that the term says that anything that happens, happens for a reason. "Sufficient reason" is also known as the "Causal Doctrine." Why do we have seasons? We have seasons because the Earth is tilted. At one point of its orbit around the Sun, one part of the Earth is closer to the Sun and it is summer there. Six months later, another part of the Earth is closer to the Sun, and it is summer there.

*The Stanford Encyclopedia of Philosophy* states, "The Principle of Sufficient Reason is a powerful and controversial philosophical principle stipulating that everything must have a reason, cause, or ground."

https://plato.stanford.edu/entries/sufficient-reason/

**Why did Voltaire choose the names *Candide, Cunegonde,* and *Pangloss* for his main characters?**

*Candide*

- Candide is candid. He is open and frank and naive and trusting.
- "Candide" is from the French and means "pure, innocent, naive."
- The word "candid" means these things:

1. Free from prejudice; impartial.

2. Characterized by openness and sincerity of expression; unreservedly straightforward: In private, I gave them my candid opinion.

3. Not posed or rehearsed: a candid snapshot.

Source: *The American Heritage® Dictionary of the English Language*, Fourth Edition

Copyright © 2000 by Houghton Mifflin Company.

2. Free from undue bias; disposed to think and judge according to truth and justice, or without partiality or prejudice; fair; just; impartial; as, a candid opinion.

3. Open; frank; ingenuous; outspoken.

Source: *Webster's Revised Unabridged Dictionary*, © 1996, 1998 MICRA, Inc.

*Cunegonde*

• This name makes me think of Come and Gone. Cunegonde goes out of and comes into the short novel. However, according to <http://i-am-pregnant.com/names/girls/Cunegonde>, which I accessed on 24 April 2009, Cunegonde is a French name for females. It means "brave war," which is an ironic choice for her name because there is nothing brave about war in this satire.

*Pangloss*

• Pangloss is a philosopher.

• Pan: can mean everything.

• Gloss: can mean an explanation.

• Pangloss the philosopher tries to explain everything.

• In Greek, the name means "all tongue." We can think of Pangloss as being basically "all talk." Pangloss does talk a lot.

**Why did Voltaire choose the name *Baron Thunder-ten-tronckh* (17)? Why is the Baron important?**

• Voltaire is making fun of long, pretentious German names.

• The Baron is important because his castle has a door and windows. Of course, the Baron also has a title. However, the title is hereditary. It was not earned through merit.

• The Baron is not important because of any personal merit that we are aware of.

• Voltaire makes fun of the Baron because the Baron has an inflated sense of self-esteem. Voltaire also makes fun of a society that regards the Baron as being important.

**If you have read *Candide* before, identify its theme. (Also: define *theme*.)**

• *Candide* tries to answer this question: What is the best way to live in a world that is filled with evil?

- This is a definition of "theme":

THEME: A central idea or statement that unifies and controls the entire work. The theme can take the form of a brief and meaningful insight or a comprehensive vision of life; it may be a single idea such as "progress" (in many Victorian works), "order and duty" (in many early Roman works), "seize-the-day" (in many late Roman works), or "jealousy" (in Shakespeare's *Othello*). The theme may also be a more complicated doctrine, such as Milton's theme in *Paradise Lost*, "to justify the ways of God to men," or "Socialism is the only sane reaction to the labor abuses in Chicago meat-packing plants" (Upton Sinclair's *The Jungle*). A theme is the author's way of communicating and sharing ideas, perceptions, and feelings with readers, and it may be directly stated in the book, or it may only be implied. Compare with *motif* and *leit-motif*.

Source: http://guweb2.gonzaga.edu/faculty/wheeler/lit_terms_T.html.

# Chapter 2: "What happened to Candide among the Bulgars."

**What evil does Candide come across in this chapter? Does this kind of evil still exist today?**

*The Draft (Conscription)*

• Candide is drafted into the army without giving his permission.

• In the United States today, we have a volunteer army; however, that may change in the future.

• The draft in *Candide* is worse than the draft that could be implemented in the United States. Basically, the military officers in *Candide* simply find men and draft them. They tell them to drink to a King's health, and then they tell them that they have volunteered to serve in the King's army.

• At one time people would be gotten drunk. When they woke up, they would find themselves out at sea. They had no choice but to work as sailors. This act is called "Shanghaiing" someone. This is a form of kidnapping. People were also forced to serve as soldiers.

*Military Discipline and Punishment*

• The military discipline and punishment is severe. Candide is taught to drill, and he is beaten when he does not perform the drill well.

• When Candide deserts the army (because of a belief in free will), he is captured and given his choice of either receiving 12 bullets in the brain or running a gauntlet of 2,000 men 36 times. He runs the gauntlet twice and is beaten so badly that he prefers the 12 bullets in the brain. Fortunately, the King of the Bulgars pardons him.

**A note on p. 121 of the Bantam edition says, "The Bulgars ... represent the Prussians, and Avars the French, who fought each other during the Seven Years' War, which was in progress as Voltaire wrote *Candide*." If you feel like doing research, give information about the Seven Years' War. (Avoid plagiarism — don't simply**

**download information; instead, put the information in your own words and tell the source of information you used.)**

Note: Some translations use "Avars," and some translations use "Abares."

• The Bulgars represent the Prussians; the Avars represent the French.

• The Prussians and the French fought the Seven Years' War, which lasted from 1756-1763. (*Candide* was first published in January 1759.) Candide was born in Westphalia, and he is drafted there. Part of the Seven Years' War was fought in Westphalia. *Candide* is not entirely historical, nor did Voltaire intend it to be. Candide is involved in the Seven Years' War, yet he later witnesses the 1755 Lisbon Earthquake.

• Like most wars, this war was a power struggle. The major European powers, including Great Britain, were involved in it. As so often, France and Great Britain opposed each other.

• Great Britain and Prussia were on one side. France, Austria, Russia, and Sweden were on the other side. Other countries were also involved. (Spain joined with France and the other countries after 1762.)

• The French and Indian War in America was a part of the power struggle of the Seven Years' War.

**Candide is cured with the "emollients prescribed by Dioscorides" (22). Who was Dioscorides? (Avoid plagiarism — don't simply download information; instead, put the information in your own words and tell the source of information you used.)**

• Dioscorides was a 1st century CE Greek physician who traveled with the Roman army, working as a surgeon.

• Emollients are medicines for the skin. By running the gauntlet twice, Candide has been flayed — his skin has been torn from his body.

• Dioscorides wrote a book on medicine: *The Greek Herbal of Dioscorides*. This book was a standard reference for centuries, indicating the slow progress that was being made in medicine in those centuries.

**How does Voltaire satirize army life?**

• Satire is humorous criticism. Capital punishment can be a part of Army life. A deserter can be condemned to death. Here one penalty for desertion is "twelve bullets in the brain" (22). This is definitely exaggeration.

• By the way, the last American soldier to be shot for desertion was Private Eddie Slovik in World War II.

• We also see a satire on conscription — being forced to join the Army. Candide is asked to drink to the King's health, and after he does so, he is informed that he has volunteered for the King's Army.

• Satire can be both particular and universal. The Prussians were known for their harsh military training methods, and those are satirized here, but the satire comes through even for readers who don't realize that Voltaire is satirizing the Prussians.

# Chapter 3: "How Candide escaped from the Bulgars, and what happened to him."

**How does Voltaire satirize religious hypocrisy in this chapter? (The kings have "*Te Deum*" sung in their camps. By the way, what is the "*Te Deum*"?)**

• In this chapter, as in many chapters, Voltaire satirizes religious hypocrisy.

• Basically, the two kings and their armies commit many, many atrocities, then they have "*Te Deum*" sung in their camps.

• "*Te Deum*" is short for "*Te Deum Laudamus*," which is Latin for "O God, we praise you."

• "*Te Deum*" is a Christian hymn that gives thanks to God. Both armies sing the "*Te Deum*," but both armies could not have won the battle, although both armies' commanders would like their armies to think they won the battle. That would be good for morale.

• This is an English translation of the Latin words of the "*Te Deum*":

> We praise Thee, O God: we acknowledge Thee to be the Lord.
> All the earth doth worship Thee and the Father everlasting.
> To Thee all Angels:
> To Thee the heavens and all the Powers therein.
> To Thee the Cherubim and Seraphim cry with unceasing voice:
> Holy, Holy, Holy: Lord God of Hosts.
> The heavens and the earth are full of the majesty of Thy glory.
> Thee the glorious choir of the Apostles.
> Thee the admirable company of the Prophets.
> Thee the white-robed army of Martyrs praise.

Thee the Holy Church throughout all the world doth acknowledge.
The Father of infinite Majesty.
Thine adorable, true and only Son
Also the Holy Ghost the Paraclete.
Thou art the King of Glory, O Christ.
Thou art the everlasting Son of the Father.
Thou having taken upon Thee to deliver man
didst not abhor the Virgin's womb.
Thou having overcome the sting of death
didst open to believers the kingdom of heaven.
Thou sittest at the right hand of God
in the glory of the Father.
We believe that Thou shalt come to be our Judge.
We beseech Thee, therefore, help Thy servants:
whom Thou has redeemed with Thy precious Blood.
Make them to be numbered with Thy Saints in glory everlasting.
Lord, save Thy people:
and bless Thine inheritance.
Govern them and lift them up forever.
Day by day we bless Thee.
And we praise Thy name forever:
and world without end.
Vouchsafe, O Lord, this day to keep us without sin.
Have mercy on us, O Lord: have mercy on us.
Let Thy mercy, O Lord, be upon us:
as we have hoped in Thee.
O Lord, in Thee have I hoped:
let me never be confounded.
Source:
http://www.chantcd.com/lyrics/we_praise_thee.htm

**How does Candide escape from the Bulgars?**

• Candide deserts.

• Previously, Candide deserted, and he had been caught and punished. This time, however, he is luckier. This time, he escapes successfully. One reason he escapes successfully is that so many soldiers have died in battle.

**Is war noble, according to this short novel? How does Voltaire satirize war? What war atrocities are committed in this chapter?**

• War is horrible, according to this short novel.

• The soldiers, of course, kill each other. In the battle, perhaps 30,000 soldiers died.

• Many atrocities are committed. For one thing, civilians are hurt on both sides.

• The Bulgars destroy an Avar village, killing and raping, and then killing the raped women. The Avars do exactly the same thing to a Bulgar village.

• People who have been horribly burned are shrieking to be put to death to end their misery and pain.

**If you feel like doing research, pick any historical war and describe a few atrocities that were committed in it.**

• Wars are excellent opportunities to commit atrocities.

• The My Lai (Mee Leye) atrocity occurred when United States soldiers massacred Vietnamese civilians.

• Lt. William L. Calley led his soldiers to My Lai on March 16, 1968, where they massacred 347 unarmed civilians — men, women, and children. A soldier wrote letters to government officials, and the House of Representatives investigated and concluded that yes, a massacre had taken place. William L. Calley was convicted and sentenced to life imprisonment, but he was later paroled.

**How does Voltaire satirize religious hypocrisy in this chapter? How do the charitable Christians of Holland treat Candide? (By the way, the contents of a full what are poured on Candide's head?)**

• The charitable Christians of Holland do NOT behave like charitable Christians.

• Candide asks for alms, but the people tell him that he will be locked up if he continues to bother them.

• An orator who has spoken about charity for a whole hour scowls when Candide asks for alms, then asks if Candide believes that the Pope is the Antichrist. Hearing that Candide has not heard that the Pope is the Antichrist, the orator declares that Candide does not deserve to eat.

• A woman pours the contents of a full chamberpot on Candide's head.

# Chapter 4: "How Candide met his former philosophy teacher, Dr. Pangloss, and what ensued."

**Write a brief character analysis of James the Anabaptist. What is an Anabaptist? What is Anabaptism?**

- In some translations, James is called Jacques.
- The Christians in Holland talk about Christian charity, but James the Anabaptist actually practices it.
- James the Anabaptist gives Candide some money (two florins) and offers to give him a job. He also washes him and feeds him bread and beer.
- An Anabaptist follows the tenets of Anabaptism.
- An Anabaptist believes in adult, rather than infant, baptism. Anabaptists believe that infants and children cannot yet understand Christian teachings, and so they ought not to be baptized. The Anabaptists were persecuted, so they took refuge in Holland, which was mainly religiously tolerant, although we see in *Candide* some Dutch who are not religiously tolerant.
- Anabaptists also rejected worldly amusements and holding public office.
- Apparently, Voltaire is very sympathetic to the Anabaptists.
- James the Anabaptist takes care of people, unlike some hypocritical Dutch people. Also, James is not like the soldiers, who kill and rape other people.
- In Chapter 4, James the Anabaptist helps Dr. Pangloss by feeding him and having him cured of syphilis. James also makes Pangloss his bookkeeper.
- The Dutch preacher talks about charity, but James the Anabaptist actually practices charity.
- We see much evil in *Candide*, but here we see an example of good.

• James is a model whom we can follow. James recognizes that many human beings have grave faults, yet he acts to help other people. James is a good man. James is both a thinker and a doer. He thinks about human nature, and he fights against evil.

• We can compare the story of James the Anabaptist to Jesus' parable of the Good Samaritan. The Samaritans were looked down on, but the Good Samaritan took care of a man who needed help. The Anabaptists were looked down on, but James the Anabaptist takes care of people who need help: Candide and Dr. Pangloss.

• **Retell in your own words Jesus' parable of the Good Samaritan (Luke 20:25-37). What is a parable?**

• This is the parable of the Good Samaritan in Luke 10:25-37 (King James Version):

> *25:* And, behold, a certain lawyer stood up, and tempted him, saying, Master, what shall I do to inherit eternal life?

> *26:* He said unto him, What is written in the law? how readest thou?

> *27:* And he answering said, Thou shalt love the Lord thy God with all thy heart, and with all thy soul, and with all thy strength, and with all thy mind; and thy neighbour as thyself.

> *28:* And he said unto him, Thou hast answered right: this do, and thou shalt live.

> *29:* But he, willing to justify himself, said unto Jesus, And who is my neighbour?

> *30:* And Jesus answering said, A certain man went down from Jerusalem to Jericho, and fell among thieves, which

stripped him of his raiment, and wounded him, and departed, leaving him half dead.

*31:* And by chance there came down a certain priest that way: and when he saw him, he passed by on the other side.

*32:* And likewise a Levite, when he was at the place, came and looked on him, and passed by on the other side.

*33:* But a certain Samaritan, as he journeyed, came where he was: and when he saw him, he had compassion on him,

*34:* And went to him, and bound up his wounds, pouring in oil and wine, and set him on his own beast, and brought him to an inn, and took care of him.

*35:* And on the morrow when he departed, he took out two pence, and gave them to the host, and said unto him, Take care of him; and whatsoever thou spendest more, when I come again, I will repay thee.

*36:* Which now of these three, thinkest thou, was neighbour unto him that fell among the thieves?

*37:* And he said, He that shewed mercy on him. Then said Jesus unto him, Go, and do thou likewise.

• A parable is a short tale that teaches a moral or a religious lesson. Parables differ from fables in that parables usually feature human beings while fables usually feature animals.

**What has happened to Cunegonde?**

• She is supposedly dead.

• Pangloss says that she was raped as much as any woman can be raped by Bulgarian soldiers, then she was supposedly disemboweled.

Later, Cunegonde will admit to being raped by only one soldier, but she may be lying.

• The Bulgarian soldiers also killed Cunegonde's mother, attacked the Baron, destroyed the animals, the barn, and the trees.

• The Bulgarian soldiers also treated Cunegonde's brother the same way they treated Cunegonde. In other words, they raped him and then supposedly killed him.

• Pangloss says that Cunegonde and the Baron's family have been revenged because the Abar soldiers did the same things to a neighboring barony that was owned by a Baron who supported the Bulgars. In other words, both sides are committing atrocities against civilians.

• From *Candide*:

As soon as Pangloss had a little refreshed himself, Candide began to repeat his inquiries concerning Miss Cunegund. "She is dead," replied the other. "Dead!" cried Candide, and immediately fainted away; his friend restored him by the help of a little bad vinegar, which he found by chance in the stable. Candide opened his eyes, and again repeated: "Dead! is Miss Cunegund dead? Ah, where is the best of worlds now? But of what illness did she die? Was it of grief on seeing her father kick me out of his magnificent castle?" "No," replied Pangloss, "her body was ripped open by the Bulgarian soldiers, after they had subjected her to as much cruelty as a damsel could survive; they knocked the Baron, her father, on the head for attempting to defend her; my lady, her mother, was cut in pieces; my poor pupil was served just in the same manner as his sister, and as for the castle, they have not left one stone upon another; they have destroyed all the ducks, and the sheep, the barns, and the trees; but we have had our revenge, for the Abares have done the very same thing in a neighboring barony, which belonged to a Bulgarian lord."

(Translation by Tobias Smollett)

**What has happened to Dr. Pangloss? What role does syphilis play in this chapter? (By the way, what is syphilis?)**
• Pangloss is in a terrible condition — he says that he is dying — because he caught syphilis from Paquette.
• Fortunately, James has him cured of syphilis.
• Pangloss loses an eye and an ear, but his mind is sound, and he becomes James' bookkeeper.
• Syphilis is a sexually transmitted disease that can kill if left untreated. Mothers can also transmit the disease to their unborn children.
• Back when *Candide* was written, syphilis was referred to as the pox.
• Christopher Columbus was blamed for bringing syphilis to Europe, but probably Christopher Columbus brought syphilis to the New World from Europe.
• From *Candide*:

"O my dear Candide, you must remember Pacquette, that pretty wench, who waited on our noble Baroness; in her arms I tasted the pleasures of Paradise, which produced these Hell torments with which you see me devoured. She was infected with an ailment, and perhaps has since died of it; she received this present of a learned Franciscan, who derived it from the fountainhead; he was indebted for it to an old countess, who had it of a captain of horse, who had it of a marchioness, who had it of a page, the page had it of a Jesuit, who, during his novitiate, had it in a direct line from one of the fellow adventurers of Christopher Columbus; for my part I shall give it to nobody, I am a dying man."

(Translation by Tobias Smollett)

• In some translations, "Pacquette" becomes "Paquette." Lowell Bair uses "Paquette." Some translations use "Cunegonde"; other translations use "Cunegund."

# Chapter 5: "Storm, shipwreck and earthquake, and what happened to Dr. Pangloss, Candide and James the Anabaptist."

- **Write a brief character analysis of the sailor.**

  - The sailor is evil.

  - Without even looking at him, the sailor lets James the Anabaptist drown even though James the Anabaptist had saved the sailor's life.

  - The sailor is made happy by the earthquake because he will get something out of it for himself.

  - The sailor risks his life to get money, and then gets drunk. Then he sobers up and pays a prostitute to have sex with him.

  - The sailor claims to have trampled a cross four times in Japan. The Japanese did not want to deal with Christians, so they made traders trample a cross before they would deal with them.

  **Compare and contrast the sailor and James the Anabaptist, and the sailor and Pangloss.**

  - As we have seen, the sailor is evil.

  - James the Anabaptist is good.

  - James the Anabaptist works to keep the ship afloat and works to save the cruel and brutal sailor — even though the sailor had hit him.

  - One thing we learn is that bad thing things can happen to good people, and good things — such as staying alive — can happen to bad people who do not deserve it.

  - The sailor is evil because he is indifferent to the suffering of others and because he does not work to relieve that suffering. James the Anabaptist is good because he cares about other people, and he works to relieve the suffering of other people.

  - The sailor is a foil to James the Anabaptist. Here are a couple of definitions of "foil":

A character that serves by contrast to highlight or emphasize opposing traits in another character. For instance, in the film *Chasing Amy*, the character Silent Bob is a foil for his partner, Jake [sic; should be "Jay"], who is loquacious and foul-mouthed. In Shakespeare's *Hamlet*, Laertes the man of action is a foil to the reluctant Hamlet. The angry hothead Hotspur in *Henry IV, Part I,* is the foil to the cool and calculating Prince Hal.

Source: http://guweb2.gonzaga.edu/faculty/wheeler/lit_terms_F.html

A foil is a character whose personality and attitude is opposite the personality and attitude of another character. Because these characters contrast, each makes the personality of the other stand out. In Sophocles' *Antigone*, Ismene is a foil for Antigone. Where Antigone is aware of the world, Ismene denies knowledge and hides from it. Where Antigone stands up to authority, Ismene withers before it. Antigone is active and Ismene is passive. Ismene's presence in the play highlights the qualities Antigone will display in her conflict with Creon making her an excellent foil.

Source:

http://masconomet.org/teachers/trevenen/litterms.htm#F

**If you feel like doing research, explain what happened in the great Lisbon earthquake of 1755.**

• On November 1, 1755, the great Lisbon earthquake occurred, killing more than 30,000 people. What makes the great Lisbon earthquake so notable is that many of the dead were in church at the time of the earthquake, celebrating the feast of All Saints Day. This is ironic. People may suppose that God would take care of good people and of people who worship Him, but that obviously is not the case, at least insofar as not being killed in an earthquake is concerned.

• Voltaire wrote a poem titled "Poem on the Disaster of Lisbon," in which he questioned philosophical optimism.

• So much death and suffering made people question philosophical optimism. With all this death and suffering, can this really be the best of all possible worlds?

**What kind of evil do we see in Chapter 5? What kind of evil did we see in Chapter 3? What is the difference between natural evil and moral evil?**

• Two main kinds of evil exist:

1) Natural evil. (Or physical evil.) The Lisbon earthquake is an act of Nature.

2) Moral evil. War and the slaughter and rape of innocent civilians are evils created by Humankind.

• In Chapter 3, we saw moral evil — man-made evil. War is an evil that Humankind, not nature — is responsible for.

• In Chapter 5, we see both kinds of evil. The Lisbon earthquake is an example of natural evil. However, the evil sailor is an example of moral evil.

• The results of the two kinds of evil are very similar. In the war between Abars and the Bulgars, innocent people are injured and killed. In the Great Lisbon Earthquake, innocent people are injured and killed. Both kinds of evil end with injured and dying and dead people lying among wreckage.

**Are natural disasters punishment for moral evil, according to this chapter?**

• Some people think that natural evil is a punishment for immoral behavior. For example, some people think that homosexuality is a sin; therefore, God sent AIDS to punish homosexuals. However, this is not so. AIDS-infected babies exist, and people have gotten AIDS from transfusions. The babies are certainly innocent of being homosexuals, as are many or most of the people who got AIDS from blood transfusions.

• In this chapter, James the good Anabaptist dies, but the brutal sailor survives.

• In this chapter, the first living person met after the Lisbon earthquake is a prostitute whom the sailor pays money so he can have sex with her.

• If the earthquake had been sent to punish the guilty, why does James the Anabaptist die and the sailor live?

**Two ways of explaining the Great Lisbon Earthquake are 1) it is punishment for our sins, and 2) it is for the greater good. Is either of these explanations satisfactory?**

• The explanation that the Great Lisbon Earthquake is punishment for our sins is not satisfactory because good people die in the earthquake, while evil people are still alive after the earthquake.

• The explanation that the Great Lisbon Earthquake is for the greater good is probably unsatisfactory for most people. Should non-volunteers die for the greater good? None of the people who died in the Great Lisbon Earthquake volunteered to die. Of course, we can also ask what that greater good would be. Much of Lisbon was leveled and had to be rebuilt. Is it right that so many people had to die so that other people could get jobs rebuilding the city?

**Do good people exist in the world, according to *Candide*?**

• Very definitely, both evil and good people exist, according to Candide. We have already seen that James the Anabaptist is a very good man. Following the Great Lisbon Earthquake, many good people —

not the sailor, of course — work together to help the injured. This, of course, helps to relieve the suffering, although much suffering remains.

• As a young child, TV's Mister Rogers would sometimes watch the news, which of course often reported on many horrifying events. Whenever the young Mister Rogers was upset by what he saw, his mother would tell him, "Look for the helpers. You will always find people who are helping." (Source: Fred Rogers, *The World According to Mister Rogers*, p. 187.)

• From *Candide*:

Candide fainted away, and Pangloss fetched him some water from a neighboring spring. The next day, in searching among the ruins, they found some eatables with which they repaired their exhausted strength. After this they assisted the inhabitants in relieving the distressed and wounded. Some, whom they had humanely assisted, gave them as good a dinner as could be expected under such terrible circumstances. The repast, indeed, was mournful, and the company moistened their bread with their tears; but Pangloss endeavored to comfort them under this affliction by affirming that things could not be otherwise than they were.

(Translation by Tobias Smollett)

**• In Chapter 3, Pangloss asked Candide for help. In Chapter 5, Candide asks Pangloss for help. Compare and contrast how the two men respond to the requests for help.**

• Pangloss sometimes acts like the sailor in that he does not help Candide when Candide needs help. One difference between the two is that the sailor actively does evil, while Pangloss talks instead of taking action to help other people. Either way, Voltaire prefers that action be taken to help people who are suffering.

• In Chapter 3, Candide ran across Pangloss, who was starving. Candide immediately got food for him, although Candide really wanted to hear what had happened to Cunegonde. In contrast, in Chapter 5, Candide needs and requests help from Pangloss, who keeps on talking and philosophizing until Candide faints — then Pangloss fetches him some water.

• One thing we can learn is that often action is preferable to talk. When people need help, take action.

# Chapter 6: "How a fine auto-da-fé was performed to prevent earthquakes, and how Candide was flogged."

**What is an auto-da-fé? Why do the authorities wish to hold an auto-da-fé? Does the auto-da-fé work?**

• The Inquisition used to pass sentences on people they thought were heretics. Both the announcement in public of these sentences and the execution in public sentences are known as auto-da-fés.

• The authorities wish to hold an auto-da-fé because they believe that it is an infallible means of preventing earthquakes.

• No, the auto-da-fé does not work. Candide is beaten, a couple of people who would not eat pork are burned to death, and Pangloss is hung, but the auto-da-fé is immediately followed by another earthquake.

• The auto-da-fé is an example of superstition.

• Often, such things as public executions are entertainment for spectators. For example, in Mark Twain's *The Adventures of Tom Sawyer*, people attend the funeral of Injun Joe and think that they are nearly as entertained as they would have been at the hanging. The auto-da-fé is also an entertainment for the spectators. In the next chapter, we find that refreshments were served in between the Mass and the executions (35-36).

• By the way, "auto-da-fé" is Portuguese for "act of faith."

• The most usual form of execution at an auto-da-fé was burning at the stake.

• I downloaded this information from http://www.bartleby.com/81/1099.html on June 18, 2004:

E. Cobham Brewer 1810–1897. *Dictionary of Phrase and Fable*. 1898.

Auto da Fe. [An act of faith.]

A day set apart by the Inquisition for the examination of "heretics." Those not acquitted were burnt. The reason why inquisitors burnt their victims was, because they are forbidden to "shed blood"; an axiom of the Roman Catholic Church being, *Eccle'sia non novit san'guinem*" (the church is untainted with blood).

• A number of people are punished at the auto-da-fé:

Pangloss: The Inquisition thinks that Pangloss doesn't believe in free will.

Candide: The Inquisition thinks that Candide agrees with Pangloss.

A Biscayan: He married his godmother. The Church did not allow such marriages.

Two men who are guilty of refusing to eat pork: This marks the men as Jews. In 1492, Spain and Portugal expelled unconverted Jews. Some Jews pretended to convert, but remained Jews. These men are two of those Jews.

• Pangloss is hanged — something that is not customary at auto-da-fés. We will see later the reason for this.

• Lots of irony takes place at the auto-da-fé:

• The auto-da-fé is held to prevent earthquakes, but another earthquake takes place after the auto-da-fé.

• A Mass is held at the auto-da-fé. Anyone who believes in a loving God will find that ironic. A sermon is also preached.

• Beautiful music is played at the auto-da-fé. We think of auto-da-fés as barbaric, and we think of beautiful music as civilized. It is ironic that music is played at the auto-da-fé.

• Here is a definition of "Irony":

1a. The use of words to express something different from and often opposite to their literal meaning. b. An expression or utterance marked by a deliberate contrast between apparent and intended meaning. c. A literary style employing such contrasts for humorous or rhetorical effect. See synonyms at wit1. 2a. Incongruity between what might be expected and what actually occurs: *"Hyde noted the irony of Ireland's copying the nation she most hated"* (Richard Kain). b. An occurrence, result, or circumstance notable for such incongruity. 3. Dramatic irony. 4. Socratic irony.

Source: *The American Heritage® Dictionary of the English Language*: Fourth Edition. 2000.

• From *Candide*:

After the earthquake, which had destroyed three-fourths of the city of Lisbon, the sages of that country could think of no means more effectual to preserve the kingdom from utter ruin than to entertain the people with an auto-da-fé, it having been decided by the University of Coimbra, that the burning of a few people alive by a slow fire, and with great ceremony, is an infallible preventive of earthquakes.

(Translation by Tobias Smollett)

• In Portugal, Coimbra was the center of the Inquisition.

**If you feel like doing research, explain some historical examples of auto-da-fé.**

• The first auto-da-fé was held on February 12, 1481, in Seville, Spain:

Six Marrano men and six women were burned alive for allegedly practicing Judaism. The Auto da Fe (Act of Faith) combined the Judicial ceremony of the Inquisition with vociferous sermons. An individual could be denounced for having lapsed back into his old religion or committing heresy. Although the Inquisition and the Auto da Fe was used on anyone accused of heresy, its main victims were Jews. The inquisition accused people of backsliding or heresy for actions such as not eating pig (for whatever reason), washing hands before prayer, changing clothes on the Sabbath, etc. Over two thousand Auto da Fes are said to have taken place in the Iberian Peninsula and its colonies. The number of victims in Spain alone is estimated at 39,912, many of whom were burned alive. Some were burned in effigy. Others, convicted posthumously, were dug up and burned — and the property they left was confiscated from their heirs. Approximately 340,000 people, many of them Jews, suffered at the hands of the Inquisition, although the vast majority were given lesser punishments. The last Auto da Fe was held in 1790.

Source:

http://jewishhistory.org.il/
history.php?startyear=1480&endyear=1489

Date Downloaded: 20 December 2008

• Of course, many other auto-da-fés were held:

*1486 February 12, AUTO DA FE AT TOLEDO (Spain)*

The first in that city and one of the most lenient Auto da Fes anywhere. The Jews were forced to recant, fined 1/5 of their property and permanently forbidden to wear decent clothes or hold office.

*1486 December 10, AUTO DA FE AT TOLEDO (Spain)*

This time more than 900 people were persecuted and humiliated at the Auto da Fe. Though many suffered on the forced penitential marches, no one was actually killed.

Source:                                    http://jewishhistory.org.il/history.php?startyear=1480&endyear=1489

Date Downloaded: 20 December 2008

**If you feel like doing research, explain what was the Spanish Inquisition.**
• The Inquisition's purpose was to investigate heresy. It was a Tribunal of the Roman Catholic Church. (Protestantism had not yet started.)
• The Medieval Inquisition is separate from the Spanish Inquisition. In the early Middle Ages, bishops had the duty to investigate heresy. In 1233, Pope Gregory IX, alarmed by the heresy of Albigensianism, established a papal Inquisition. Pope Gregory IX sent Dominican friars to investigate heresy in southern France.
• In 1478, Ferdinand and Isabella of Spain established the Spanish Inquisition. Tomas de Torquemada was an early leader. The main purpose of the Spanish Inquisition was to discover so-called "converts" to Christianity who still practiced their Jewish or Muslim religions.

However, soon many, many people were investigated by the Spanish Inquisition, including St. Ignatius of Loyola and St. Theresa of Ávila, both of whom were suspected of being heretics. The Spanish Inquisition resulted in the deaths of many people in auto-da-fés. In 1834, the Spanish Inquisition was abolished.

• Of course, this chapter is set in Portugal, not Spain.

**Identify some forms of superstitions that exist today. What is the danger of believing in superstitions?**

• Some kinds of superstition are basically benign. For example, you may believe that if you wear your red sweater on the day of an important game, you will help your favorite sports team to win.

• Others can be more dangerous. For example, a belief in astrology. No one should allow astrology to rule his or her life.

• One danger of superstition is that it can keep us from being scientific. Another is that it can keep you from using your free will.

# Chapter 7: "How an old woman took care of Candide, and how he found the object of his love."

**What do we learn about the old woman in this chapter?**

• The old woman is apparently kind. (We should note that good people exist in *Candide*.)

• The old woman gives Candide shelter, food and drink, and an ointment for his back. The old woman, we will see, has suffered, and here she helps to relieve the suffering of Candide.

• When Candide wants to thank the old woman by kissing her hand, she says that he should not kiss *her* hand, implying that he should kiss the hand of another person.

• Of course, we soon find that the old woman is the servant of Cunegonde.

• The old woman will be an advisor for both Candide and Cunegonde.

• Later, the old woman will tell her story, which is parallel to the story of Cunegonde.

• The old woman is very practical. She is aware of the evil in life. The old woman has common sense.

**Among other things, *Candide* is a parody of the romantic adventure story. How is the romantic adventure story parodied in this chapter?**

• Romantic adventure stories have a few clichés, as do picaresque novels. One of them is a recognition scene. Here we have a mysterious old woman, a remote house, and a veiled woman. Candide lifts the veil of the woman and discovers that she is Cunegonde.

• *Candide* will have a number of recognition scenes. Many people who are thought to be dead will turn out to be alive.

• Note a little humor here. When Candide recognizes Cunegonde, both of them fall. Candide falls down on the hard floor at Cunegonde's feet, but Cunegonde wisely falls on the soft couch.

40

# Chapter 8: "Cunegonde's story."

**What is Cunegonde's story?**

- Cunegonde has suffered much injustice:

  - She says that a Bulgar soldier raped and stabbed her. Earlier, Pangloss had said that many soldiers raped her.

  - Cunegonde lived for a while with a Bulgar captain who killed the Bulgar soldier who raped Cunegonde — not because of the rape, but because the soldier did not salute him while the soldier was busily raping Cunegonde.

  - The Bulgar captain soon sold Cunegonde to a Jew named Don Issachar. He keeps her in this house.

  - The Grand Inquisitor saw Cunegonde, desired her, and now forces the Jew to share Cunegonde with him. Of course, the Grand Inquisitor could easily have the Jew killed in an auto-da-fé.

  - Cunegonde says that she has not slept with either man. (Later, in Chapter 13, the old woman says that both men have enjoyed Cunegonde's favors.)

  - Note that Jews can be as immoral as Christians. Both the Jew and the Grand Inquisitor are using Cunegonde as a sex slave.

**Write brief character analyses of Don Issachar and the Grand Inquisitor.**

• Don Issachar and the Grand Inquisitor are not nice people. They do not mind taking advantage of a woman. They take care of Cunegonde, but only because they want to enjoy her sexually.

• The Grand Inquisitor is a religious hypocrite. He holds an auto-da-fé in which three people die (and two others — Candide and Pangloss — are hurt) because he wishes to intimidate Don Issachar into sharing Cunegonde with him.

• The Jew is named Don Issachar. Issachar in the Bible is the son of Jacob and Leah. He is also one of the ancestors of the 12 tribes.

• I downloaded this information from http://www.bartleby.com/65/is/Issachar.html on June 24, 2004:

**Issachar**

in the patriarchal narratives of the Bible, son of Jacob and Leah and the ancestor of one of the 12 tribes. The territory allotted to the tribe of Issachar at the time of the conquest extended along the west bank of the Jordan.

*The Columbia Encyclopedia*, Sixth Edition. Copyright © 2003 Columbia University Press.

**Why was the auto-da-fé held (two purposes)?**

• We find out that there were actually two purposes of the auto-da-fé:

1) As we have learned before, one purpose was to prevent future earthquakes.

2) The second purpose was that the Grand Inquisitor wished to intimidate Don Issachar, the Jew. The message was either share Cunegonde with me or suffer an auto-da-fé. Because Don Issachar is a Jew, the Grand Inquisitor can easily put him to death.

• Of course we see an example of religious hypocrisy here in the form of the Grand Inquisitor.

43

# Chapter 9: "What happened to Cunegonde, Candide, the Grand Inquisitor and the Jew."

**Why does Candide kill Don Issachar and the Grand Inquisitor?**

• Don Issachar thinks — incorrectly — that Candide is unarmed, and he advances toward him with a dagger — because he is jealous of Cunegonde — to kill Candide. Candide kills Don Issachar in self-defense.

• The Grand Inquisitor arrives. Candide is in love with Cunegonde, he is jealous because the Grand Inquisitor wants to enjoy Cunegonde's favors, and he has been beaten in the auto-da-fé and knows that the Great Inquisitor is likely to want to burn Candide to death. Therefore, Candide kills the Grand Inquisitor.

**What is the old woman's plan?**

• She wants everyone to flee to Cadiz.

• She wants Cunegonde to gather up her gold coins and diamonds before they flee.

• The old woman is both intelligent and practical.

• By the way, we learn that the old woman has only one buttock. Of course, we wonder why she has only one buttock. Our curiosity will be satisfied in Chapter 12, when the old woman tells her story.

• Apparently, the Holy Brotherhood is an organization that tries to keep the roads safe from murderers and robbers. They chase after Candide, whom of course they regard as a murderer.

**How does Voltaire develop the theme of religious satire in this chapter?**

• Of course, both the Jew and the Grand Inquisitor are behaving immorally by keeping Cunegonde as a sex slave.

• The bodies of the Grand Inquisitor and the Jew are treated very differently. From *Candide*:

"My Lord, the Inquisitor, was interred in a magnificent manner, and Master Issachar's body was thrown upon a dunghill."

(Translation by Tobias Smollett)

• In Chapter 10, we discover that a Franciscan has stolen Cunegonde's jewels.
• In *Candide*, being moral and being religious are two very different things.

# Chapter 10: "How Candide, Cunegonde, and the old woman arrived at Cadiz in great distress, and how they set sail from there."

**What happens to Cunegonde's money and diamonds?**

• The old woman thinks that a reverend Franciscan stole the money and diamonds. He came into their room twice and left long before they did.

• Candide is upset because he thinks that the reverend Franciscan ought to have left them something so they can continue their journey.

• Fortunately, they are able to continue their journey. The old woman suggests that they sell a horse, and Candide performs his Bulgar drills and is placed in charge of a company of infantry, and they begin to sail for the new world — in particular, Paraguay.

• The Benedictines also come under fire from Voltaire. A Benedictine friar buys the horse — but for a low price.

**To where do our heroes set sail, and why?**

• They begin to sail for the new world — in particular, Paraguay.

• They sail for a few reasons:

1. They need to escape the people who will want to avenge the death of the Inquisitor General.

2. They are still searching for the best of all possible worlds. Apparently, the old world — Europe — is not it.

• From *Candide*:

Candide, Cunegund, and the old woman, after passing through Lucina, Chellas, and Letrixa, arrived at length at Cadiz. A fleet was then getting ready, and troops were assembling in order to induce the reverend fathers, Jesuits of Paraguay, who were accused of having excited one of the Indian tribes in the neighborhood of the town of the Holy Sacrament, to revolt against the Kings of Spain and Portugal.

Candide, having been in the Bulgarian service, performed the military exercise of that nation before the general of this little army with so intrepid an air, and with such agility and expedition, that he received the command of a company of foot. Being now made a captain, he embarked with Miss Cunegund, the old woman, two valets, and the two Andalusian horses, which had belonged to the Grand Inquisitor of Portugal.

(Translation by Tobias Smollett)

• The revolt mentioned in this chapter actually occurred. In Paraguay was a city called St. Sacrament. Spain wanted to transfer this city to Portugal. The Jesuit priests in St. Sacrament did not want this to happen, and they rebelled.

**How does Voltaire develop the theme of religious satire in this chapter?**

• The Franciscans, the Benedictines, and the Jesuits are all mentioned in this chapter, none of them favorably:

*The Franciscans*

A Franciscan is thought to have stolen Cunegonde's jewels.

The Franciscan came into Cunegonde's bedroom twice. Perhaps he was after more than just the jewels.

St. Francis of Assisi founded the Franciscans in the 13th century. At first, they were wandering preachers dedicated to living a life of poverty.

*The Benedictines*

A Benedictine buys a horse cheap from our heroes. We get the impression that he took advantage of our heroes when he made the deal. Sometimes, we hear of buying real estate from motivated sellers. Motivated sellers have to sell their property quickly, and therefore they often sell their property cheap. One way of looking at this is that the buyer is taking advantage of widows and orphans.

The Benedictine religious order was founded in the 6th century. Early in their history, they lived in monasteries, separate from the world.

*The Jesuits*

The Jesuits revolt in Paraguay. We will see later that they treat the natives very badly.

The Jesuits are the Society of Jesus. Founded in 1539, they were missionaries and teachers.

*Reform and Hypocrisy*

• Religious orders occasionally need to be reformed. Sometimes, religious orders drift away from their founders' ideals. Many great writers have criticized the materialism of various religious orders: Dante in *The Divine Comedy*, Boccaccio in *The Decameron*, and Chaucer in *The Canterbury Tales*.

• The Protestant Reformation occurred in the 16th century in part as a reaction to the Catholic clergy, some of whom were corrupt and materialistic.

• In Chapter 5, Voltaire criticized the fanaticism and intolerance of organized religions. In Chapter 10, Voltaire is criticizing the corruption and materialism of religious orders.

• Of course, we see hypocrisy in this chapter. What Jesus said to do is not what these religious people are doing.

# Chapter 11: "The old woman's story."

**Who is the old woman, and what is her story?**

- These are the facts of the old woman's story:

- The old woman is a daughter of Pope Urban X. However, there has been no Pope Urban X — so far. Her mother is the Princess of Palestrina.

- The old woman is now ugly — her nose touches her chin, so she has no teeth — yet she was beautiful when she was a young girl. The women who dressed and undressed her commented on her beauty.

- The old woman has become familiar with evil.

- The man to whom she was betrothed — the sovereign prince of Massa-Carrara — was murdered when he drank poison offered to him by his former mistress.

- When she was young, the old woman and her mother were captured by pirates, who stripped them and searched for diamonds in their rectums.

- She was raped by the pirate captain.

- She saw her mother and the other women murdered by the men fighting over them.

- She escaped, then was found by a man who lacks testicles. He is pressing himself against her, so if he had testicles, he too would rape her.

• The old woman has led a remarkable life, yet she thinks that there is nothing remarkable about it. She is matter of fact about her experiences. (Rape is common in this satire and in our world.)

• The old woman, when she was young, was captured, stripped naked, and then subjected to a search of the body cavity that she is least proud of. This is extraordinary, but she says matter of factly that such things are common. From *Candide*:

"The Moors presently stripped us as bare as ever we were born. My mother, my maids of honor, and myself, were served all in the same manner. It is amazing how quick these gentry are at undressing people. But what surprised me most was, that they made a rude sort of surgical examination of parts of the body which are sacred to the functions of nature. I thought it a very strange kind of ceremony; for thus we are generally apt to judge of things when we have not seen the world. I afterwards learned that it was to discover if we had any diamonds concealed. This practice had been established since time immemorial among those civilized nations that scour the seas. I was informed that the religious Knights of Malta never fail to make this search whenever any Moors of either sex fall into their hands. It is a part of the law of nations, from which they never deviate."

(Translation by Tobias Smollett)

• The old woman, when she was young, was raped by the Negro captain of the pirate ship. Such things are so common that, she says, "they are hardly worth mentioning." From *Candide*:

"As to myself, I was enchanting; I was beauty itself, and then I had my virginity. But, alas! I did not retain it long; this precious flower, which had been reserved for the lovely Prince of Massa Carrara, was cropped by the captain of the Moorish vessel, who was a hideous Negro, and thought he did me infinite honor. Indeed, both the Princess of Palestrina and myself must have had very strong constitutions to undergo all the hardships and violences we suffered before our arrival at Morocco. But I will not detain you any longer with such common things; they are hardly worth mentioning."

(Translation by Tobias Smollett)

• The old woman uses many superlatives as she tells her story. For example, she uses superlatives when she describes her beauty when she was a young woman. This is a parody of the superlatives used in Italian love poetry. From *Candide*:

"I grew up, and improved in beauty, wit, and every graceful accomplishment; and in the midst of pleasures, homage, and the highest expectations. I already began to inspire the men with love. My breast began to take its right form, and such a breast! white, firm, and formed like that of the Venus de' Medici; my eyebrows were as black as jet, and as for my eyes, they darted flames and eclipsed the luster of the stars, as I was told by the poets of our part of the world. My maids, when they dressed and undressed me, used to fall into an ecstasy in viewing me before and behind; and all the men longed to be in their places."

(Translation by Tobias Smollett)

• The old woman says that many of the things she has undergone are so commonly done that "they are hardly worth mentioning." This emphasizes the commonness of evil. Being common makes evil worse, not better. We would much prefer that evil acts were done rarely rather than commonly.

**Describe the common practices of the pirates.**

• They strip their prisoners naked. This is often done by oppressors. People who are naked are less likely to resist, perhaps because they feel vulnerable. Nazis did this. Naked people are less likely to run away.

• They search for diamonds hidden in prisoners' rectums. Remember *Pulp Fiction* and where the watch was hidden?

• They rape the women, both virgins and mothers. The old woman says that this is very, very common.

• Sexuality in an important theme in *Candide*. So is rape.

**According to *Candide*, can men be both brutes and religious?**

• Yes, the pirates are Moslems. They rape and murder, yet they say the five daily prayers.

• Note that Voltaire criticizes all religions, not just one.

• Voltaire has certainly criticized Christians. Now he criticizes Muslims. The Muslims kill and rape, and yet they never miss their five daily prayers. Supposedly, organized religion says not to kill and rape, yet the Muslims (and Christians) have no problem doing either evil act. From *Candide*:

> "My captain kept me concealed behind him, and with his drawn scimitar cut down everyone who opposed him; at length I saw all our Italian women and my mother mangled and torn in pieces by the monsters who contended for them. The captives, my companions, the Moors who took us, the soldiers, the sailors, the blacks, the whites, the mulattoes, and lastly, my captain himself, were all slain, and I remained alone expiring upon a heap of dead bodies. Similar

barbarous scenes were transacted every day over the whole country, which is of three hundred leagues in extent, and yet they never missed the five stated times of prayer enjoined by their prophet Mahomet."

(Translation by Tobias Smollett)

• Voltaire criticizes Christians in this chapter. The Knights of Malta are Christian, yet they perform the same the body cavity search that the Muslim pirates perform. From *Candide*:

"The Moors presently stripped us as bare as ever we were born. My mother, my maids of honor, and myself, were served all in the same manner. It is amazing how quick these gentry are at undressing people. But what surprised me most was, that they made a rude sort of surgical examination of parts of the body which are sacred to the functions of nature. I thought it a very strange kind of ceremony; for thus we are generally apt to judge of things when we have not seen the world. I afterwards learned that it was to discover if we had any diamonds concealed. This practice had been established since time immemorial among those civilized nations that scour the seas. I was informed that the religious Knights of Malta never fail to make this search whenever any Moors of either sex fall into their hands. It is a part of the law of nations, from which they never deviate."

(Translation by Tobias Smollett)

**What do you think of the ending of Chapter 11?**
• Voltaire ends the chapter well — with a teaser. A man finds the young girl who became an old woman and says, in Italian, "Oh, what

a misfortune to be without testicles!" Obviously, we want to learn his story.

• The old woman was once beautiful. She was so beautiful that she is even able to make a eunuch wish that he were able to rape her. (A eunuch is a castrated man.)

• The old woman's story has parallels to Cunegonde's story. Both were beautiful, and both were raped. Both have suffered misfortunes.

• In the next chapter, we will see that the old woman tells of growing old and of losing her beauty. This will happen to Cunegonde.

# Chapter 12: "Further misfortunes of the old woman."

**What is the story of the man without testicles?**

• In the previous chapter, we learned that everyone, including her mother and the Muslim pirate captain, is killed, with the sole exception of the old woman, who of course is still young at this point of her life.

• The eunuch is on top of the old woman when she awakes. He is apparently trying — unsuccessfully — to rape her.

• He is a castrato. His testicles were cut off in an attempt to keep his singing voice. This is an evil in part because some children died from the operation; it is an evil in any case because children do not make the decision to have themselves castrated, or if they do, they are not old or mature enough to make that decision. Some castrati sang religious music. They also sang opera.

• He is a diplomat. From *Candide*:

"I then related to him all that had befallen me, and he in return acquainted me with all his adventures, and how he had been sent to the court of the King of Morocco by a Christian prince to conclude a treaty with that monarch; in consequence of which he was to be furnished with military stores, and ships to destroy the commerce of other Christian governments."

(Translation by Tobias Smollett)

• He is treacherous. He says that he will help the young girl who will become the old woman return to Italy, but he sells her as a slave in Algiers. She becomes a member of the harem of a Muslim lord.

• He knew the old woman's mother because he was one of her court musicians.

• He dies of the plague in Algiers.

**If you feel like doing research, explain who were the castrati. (Do not plagiarize.)**

The castrati were singers who were castrated when they were boys so that they would not lose their high voices. People felt that the castrati, with the high voice of a boy powered by the chest of a full-grown man, was beautiful. The castrati sang opera and religious songs. The Italian Carlo Broschi Farinelli (1705-1782) was a famous castrato.

**If you feel like doing research, explain the horrors of the plague.**

• The plague is a disease that is contagious, malignant, and epidemic. It has killed many, many people throughout history.

• The bubonic plague is well known.

• Around 430 B.C. the plague struck Athens, Greece. The plague killed the great Athenian leader Pericles, as well as many members of his family.

**Why does the old woman have only one buttock? (Note: Keep related words together. Often, the word "only" modifies a number; when that is the case, it should be placed before the number. In addition, when referring to words as words, use quotation marks or italics.)**

• The old woman was forced to give up one buttock so it could be cooked for a meal for soldiers during a siege. The soldiers had already eaten two eunuch slaves.

• The old woman suffers plague and famine, among other evils such as slavery. She is sold from person to person. Eventually, she is in the harem of an aga, or local lord, in Turkey. The Russian army sets siege to the fort she is in, leading to famine. The soldiers decline to surrender, and they cut off one buttock from each of the women so that they can eat it. Among all the other evils we have seen, here we have cannibalism.

• Not all "good" people are all that good. A good man does convince the soldiers not to kill the women so that they can eat them.

Rather, he suggests a compromise: cut off one buttock from each lady and eat it. From *Candide*:

> "We had a very pious and humane man, who gave them a most excellent sermon on this occasion, exhorting them not to kill us all at once. 'Cut off only one of the buttocks of each of those ladies,' said he, 'and you will fare extremely well; if you are under the necessity of having recourse to the same expedient again, you will find the like supply a few days hence. Heaven will approve of so charitable an action, and work your deliverance.'"

(Translation by Tobias Smollett)

**If you feel like doing research, explain what it means when someone is "broken on the wheel." (Do not plagiarize.)**

• The old woman is apparently sold to another man, who ends up being broken upon the wheel.

• Here is information about what it means to be broken upon the wheel:

> Being "broken on the wheel" was one of the harshest middle age punishments. The criminal would be tied to a wagon wheel [...]. They would then be pummelled with a blunt weapon. The breaker's objective was to shatter as many bones as possible without killing. The criminal would then be left in a twisted mass to bleed to death. His remains might then be carried around the town, still tied to the wheel, as a warning to the citizenry.

Source:

http://www.saroftreve.com/home/museum/museum4.htm

**If you have read *Candide* before, explain how the old woman's fate foreshadows what will happen to Cunegonde. In addition, explain what foreshadowing is.**

• Cunegonde will soon no longer be beautiful, just like the old woman.

• Cunegonde will have to work for a living, after having been basically a harem girl, just like the old woman.

• The 6th edition of *A Handbook to Literature* by C. Hugh Holman and William Harmon defines "foreshadowing" in this way: "The presentation of material in a work in such a way that later events are prepared for" (201).

Here are a few other definitions:

Foreshadowing is the use of hints or clues to suggest what will happen later in literature.

Source:

http://www.tnellen.com/cybereng/lit_terms/
foreshadowing.html

Definition: A literary device used to hint at events that will follow later in the story, sometimes generating feelings of anxiety or suspense. Anton Chekhov once said that "if there is a gun hanging on the wall in the first act, it must fire in the last." That remark captures the essence of foreshadowing.

Source:

http://contemporarylit.about.com/library/
bldef-foreshadowing

**FORESHADOWING**: Suggesting, hinting, indicating, or showing what will occur later in a narrative. Foreshadowing often provides hints about what will happen next. For instance, a movie director might show a clip in which two parents discuss their son's leukemia. The camera briefly changes shots to do an extended close-up of a dying plant in the garden outside, or one of the parents might mention that another relative died on the same date. The perceptive audience sees the dying plant, or hears the reference to the date of death, and realizes this detail foreshadows the child's death later in the movie. Often this foreshadowing takes the form of a noteworthy coincidence or appears in a verbal echo of dialogue. Other examples of foreshadowing include the conversation and action of the three witches in Shakespeare's *Macbeth*, or the various prophecies that Oedipus hears during *Oedipus Rex*.

Source:

http://guweb2.gonzaga.edu/faculty/wheeler/
lit_terms_F.html

**Why hasn't the old woman ever committed suicide?**
• She says that she has often been tempted to commit suicide, but that she still loves life. From *Candide*:

"I have grown old in misery and disgrace, living with only one buttock, and having in perpetual remembrance that I am a Pope's daughter. I have been a hundred times upon the point of killing myself, but still I was fond of life. This ridiculous weakness is, perhaps, one of the dangerous principles implanted in our nature. For what can be more absurd than to persist in carrying a burden of which we wish to be eased? to detest, and yet to strive to preserve our existence? In a word, to caress the serpent that devours us, and hug him close to our bosoms till he has gnawed into our hearts?"

(Translation by Tobias Smollett)

• The old woman is a survivor. She has suffered much, much misfortune, but she lives to an old age. Why? One reason may be that she loves life. Another reason is that she accepts evil. The old woman is practical, has common sense, and accepts evil as a fact of life. A person who is aware that evil exists and that evil people exist may be better able to cope with evil than someone who is naïve.

# Chapter 13: "How Candide was forced to leave Cunegonde and the old woman."

**Is the old woman reliable and ethical?**

• In some ways, the old woman is reliable. She thought that a Franciscan stole Cunegonde's diamonds and money, and she is correct.

• The old woman, however, does advise Cunegonde to marry the governor, Don Fernando de Ibaraa y Figueroa y Mascarenes y Lampurdos y Suza, in Buenos Aires. She may do that because she is a survivor, and a good marriage — in terms of political connections and wealth and family — could help Cunegonde to survive. The old woman does not advise that Cunegonde marry for love. The old woman is pragmatic, not romantic.

• We can note that the old woman says that the Grand Inquisitor and the Jew have both enjoyed Cunegonde's favors, although Cunegonde had earlier told Candide that they had not. Of course, since the old woman is Cunegonde's servant, she should know.

**Write a brief character analysis of Don Fernando, aka Don Fernando de Ibaraa y Figueroa y Mascarenes y Lampurdos y Suza.**

• He is proud and haughty. People who meet him want to hit him.

• He is filled with lust. He meets Cunegonde, asks Candide if she is his wife, and when Candide says that they are engaged to be married, sends Candide off to inspect his troops, and when Candide is out of the way, tells Cunegonde that he will marry her the following day.

• By the way, "y" means "and" in Spanish. Spaniards have in their own surname both parents' last names. Voltaire exaggerates this for a humorous effect.

**Why does a little ship enter the harbor? Why is Candide forced to leave Cunegonde and the old woman?**

• Candide is forced to flee for his life. The little ship that enters the harbor is filled with police who are searching for the murderer of the Grand Inquisitor.

• From *Candide*:

> The old woman rightly guessed that the Franciscan with the long sleeves, was the person who had taken Miss Cunegund's money and jewels, while they and Candide were at Badajoz, in their flight from Lisbon. This same friar attempted to sell some of the diamonds to a jeweler, who presently knew them to have belonged to the Grand Inquisitor, and stopped them. The Franciscan, before he was hanged, acknowledged that he had stolen them and described the persons, and the road they had taken. The flight of Cunegund and Candide was already the towntalk. They sent in pursuit of them to Cadiz; and the vessel which had been sent to make the greater dispatch, had now reached the port of Buenos Ayres. A report was spread that an alcayde was going to land, and that he was in pursuit of the murderers of My Lord, the Inquisitor.

(Translation by Tobias Smollett)

Note: An alcayde is 1) a commander of a castle or fortress, or 2) the warden of a prison.

# Chapter 14: "How Candide and Cacambo were received by the Jesuits of Paraguay."

**Write a brief character analysis of Cacambo. Compare and contrast Cacambo and the old woman.**

- This is how Cacambo is introduced in the short novel:

Candide had brought with him from Cadiz such a footman as one often meets with on the coasts of Spain and in the colonies. He was the fourth part of a Spaniard, of a mongrel breed, and born in Tucuman. He had successively gone through the profession of a singing boy, sexton, sailor, monk, peddler, soldier, and lackey. His name was Cacambo; he had a great affection for his master, because his master was a very good man. He immediately saddled the two Andalusian horses.

(Translation by Tobias Smollett)

- Both Cacambo and the old woman are important advisors.
- Both Cacambo and the old woman are worldly wise and practical survivors. Here is a definition of "worldly wise":

experienced in and wise to the ways of the world
Source: wordnet.princeton.edu/perl/webwn

- Both Cacambo and the old woman are adaptable and resourceful and able to solve problems. In this chapter, Cacambo figures out that it would be wise for he and Candide to fight for, not against, the Jesuits.
- Both Cacambo and the old woman are servants.

- Both Cacambo and the old woman are not shocked by what they see. Apparently, they have experienced enough of life not to be shocked. Later, Candide will be shocked to see two girls who have taken monkeys as lovers. Cacambo will not be shocked.

- Cacambo is loyal to Candide, but the old woman may not be loyal to Candide.

**Has Candide changed since the beginning of the short novel?**

- Yes. Candide is not as naïve as he has been.

- In Chapter 13, he showed some disenchantment with Pangloss' optimistic views:

> "It is a thousand pities," said Candide, "that the sage Pangloss should have been hanged contrary to the custom of an auto-da-fé, for he would have given us a most admirable lecture on the moral and physical evil which overspreads the earth and sea; and I think I should have courage enough to presume to offer (with all due respect) some few objections."

> (Translation by Tobias Smollett)

- In Chapter 14, Candide shows that he does not have the high opinion of Westphalia that he used to have:

> "From what part of Germany do you come?" said the Jesuit.

> "From the dirty province of Westphalia," answered Candide. "I was born in the castle of Thunder-ten-tronckh."

> (Translation by Tobias Smollett)

- Candide will continue to change in the chapters set in South America.

**How does Voltaire criticize religion in this chapter?**

• Voltaire criticizes the Jesuits in this chapter: The Jesuits treat the Native Americans badly in this chapter. The Reverend father Commandant eats much better and in much more luxurious surroundings than the Native Americans. From *Candide*:

> Immediately they conducted Candide to a beautiful pavilion adorned with a colonnade of green marble, spotted with yellow, and with an intertexture of vines, which served as a kind of cage for parrots, humming birds, guinea hens, and all other curious kinds of birds. An excellent breakfast was provided in vessels of gold; and while the Paraguayans were eating coarse Indian corn out of wooden dishes in the open air, and exposed to the burning heat of the sun, the Reverend Father Commandant retired to his cool arbor.

(Translation by Tobias Smollett)

• Cacambo makes a major point about the Jesuits, who have everything while "the people have no money at all" (Smollett):

> "I was a scout in the College of the Assumption, and am as well acquainted with the new government of the Los Padres as I am with the streets of Cadiz. Oh, it is an admirable government, that is most certain! The kingdom is at present upwards of three hundred leagues in diameter, and divided into thirty provinces; the fathers there are masters of everything, and the people have no money at all; this you must allow is the masterpiece of justice and reason."

(Translation by Tobias Smollett)

• Cacambo also points out the Jesuits behave differently in Europe than they do in South America. In Europe they bless the princes they rebel against in South America:

"For my part, I see nothing so divine as the good fathers, who wage war in this part of the world against the troops of Spain and Portugal, at the same time that they hear the confessions of those very princes in Europe; who kill Spaniards in America and send them to Heaven at Madrid."

(Translation by Tobias Smollett)

• Additional satire of the Jesuits will occur in Chapter 15. Of course, one satiric point is that these men of God are making war.

**What is a Jesuit?**

• The Jesuits belong to the religious order of the Society of Jesus.

• The Jesuits are known as excellent teachers, and Voltaire himself attended a school with Jesuit educators.

• The Jesuits were missionaries, and they went to South America as missionaries.

• In 1765, the Jesuits were expelled from France. (*Candide* was published in 1759.) The Jesuits had much power, and many people thought that they had too much power.

• In 1540, the Jesuits were founded in Spain by St. Ignatius of Loyola.

**Write a brief character analysis of the commandant.**

• The commandant turns out to be German; in fact, he is Cunegonde's presumed-to-be-dead brother.

• The commandant is proud. He will speak with Candide when he finds out that he is German; however, we learn that he will not allow any Spaniard to open his mouth in his presence.

• The commandant has always been proud, and he remains proud although he has entered a religious order. One of Voltaire's satiric points is that entering a religious order does not necessarily mean that you are a good person.

**Why are the Jesuits leading a revolt?**

• Supposedly, the Jesuits are leading a revolt in the name of the Native Americans; however, the Native Americans do not care for the Jesuits.

• In this short novel, the Jesuits are leading the rebellion in order to increase their own wealth and power.

• The Native Americans in Paraguay are the servants of the Jesuits.

# Chapter 15: "How Candide killed the brother of his beloved Cunegonde."

**What is the commandant's story?**

• Like many other characters in *Candide*, the commandant was thought to be dead — killed during the war between the Bulgars and Avars. Like his sister, Cunegonde, the commandant survived the attack on their father's castle.

• The young Baron/commandant had fainted during the attack, but he revived when a Jesuit priest sprinkled holy water on him.

• The Jesuit priest made him a novice, and he went to Paraguay. There he rose through the ranks.

• Earlier, in Chapter 4, we learned that the commandant had been raped in the attack on his father's castle. Dr. Pangloss said that the soldiers treated the young Baron in the same way that they treated his sister. Cunegonde was raped, and therefore so was the commandant:

> "No," replied Pangloss, "her body was ripped open by the Bulgarian soldiers, after they had subjected her to as much cruelty as a damsel could survive; they knocked the Baron, her father, on the head for attempting to defend her; My Lady, her mother, was cut in pieces; **my poor pupil was served just in the same manner as his sister**; and as for the castle, they have not left one stone upon another; they have destroyed all the ducks, and sheep, the barns, and the trees; but we have had our revenge, for the Abares have done the very same thing in a neighboring barony, which belonged to a Bulgarian lord."

(Translation by Tobias Smollett; emphasis added)

• In addition, the Jesuit priest who takes care of the commandant does so at least in part because the commandant is so good looking:

> A Jesuit sprinkled us with some holy water, which was confounded salty, and a few drops of it went into my eyes; the father perceived that my eyelids stirred a little; he put his hand upon my breast and felt my heartbeat; upon which he gave me proper assistance, and at the end of three weeks I was perfectly recovered. You know, my dear Candide, **I was very handsome; I became still more so, and the Reverend Father Croust, superior of that house, took a great fancy to me**; he gave me the habit of the order, and some years afterwards I was sent to Rome.

(Translation by Tobias Smollett; emphasis added)

• One thing to notice about the commandant/young Baron is that homosexuality is associated with him — as is pride.

• When Candide says that he would like to marry Cunegonde, the young Baron is insulted. This shows his pride. Because Candide does not have noble birth, the young Baron does not want him to marry his sister, although Cunegonde would be happy to marry him.

• Voltaire supports a meritocracy; the young Baron supports an aristocracy.

**Why doesn't the commandant want Candide to marry his sister?**

• Candide is not of noble blood (or is of less noble blood than Cunegonde), but Cunegonde is of noble blood. The commandant is too proud to allow Candide to marry his sister.

• Candide tells the commandant that he wants to marry his sister. The commandant is insulted, the commandant slaps Candide with the flat of his sword, and Candide stabs the commandant, apparently killing him.

• Candide now must flee. Here Cacambo gives him practical, good advice. Candide puts on the commandant's Jesuit robe, and he and Cacambo flee on horseback.

**What plan do Candide and Cacambo follow after Candide apparently kills the Commandant?**

• Cacambo tells Candide to wear the clothing of the commandant and to escape on horseback. People will think that Candide is a Jesuit bearing orders, and he will cross the border before they learn of their mistake.

**How does Voltaire criticize religion in this chapter?**

• The Jesuits do not act the way that Christians ought to act. What is the most important point of the Christian religion? Possibly, it is the Golden Rule: Treat other people the way that you want them to treat you. The Jesuits do not do that in this (and the previous) chapter:

• The Jesuits should be peace loving, but they start a revolt in Paraguay. The occupations of priest and general ought to be contradictory. Religion and war ought to be contradictions in terms.

• The Jesuits should be peace loving, but the commandant slaps Candide with the flat of his sword.

• The Jesuits ought to be humble, but the commandant does not want Candide to marry Cunegonde, the commandant's sister, because of his lack of a noble birth.

• The Jesuits ought to help the poor, but the commandant eats much better than the Native Americans.

# Chapter 16: "What happened to the two travelers with two girls, two monkeys, and the savages known as the Oreillons."

**Who or what are the monkeys and their lovers? (In part, the monkeys are Voltaire's satiric portrayal of the noble savage. What is the noble savage?)**

• After escaping from the Jesuits, Candide and Cacambo run across two naked girls running away from two monkeys who are biting them on the buttocks. Candide wants to save the girls from the monkeys, so he shoots them. However, the monkeys were the lovers of the girls, and the girls mourn over the dead monkeys.

• Candide and Cacambo are captured by the Oreillons. The name can be translated as "Big Ears," and in some translations they are called the Biglugs. Here is a definition of "lug":

> A Lug (knob) is a typically flattened protuberance, a knob, or extrusion on the side of a vessel: pottery, jug, glass, vase, etc.

> Source: en.wikipedia.org/wiki/Lug_(knob)

> Date Downloaded: 22 December 2008

• The Oreillons are cannibals. They prepare to cook and eat Candide and Cacambo.

• The philosopher Jean-Jacques Rousseau wrote about the "noble savage." Unfortunately, these savages are not noble. Here Voltaire is satirizing the idea of the noble savage.

• Often, we believe that uncivilized people can be better than civilized people. This is likely to be a myth. (Why don't uncivilized people steal as much as civilized people? Perhaps uncivilized people have fewer possessions that are worth stealing.) Similarly, we can mythologize the working class. I know some members of the working class, and some of the members I know are stupid racists.

• We can see why Voltaire would want to criticize Rousseau. Rousseau believed that Humankind was basically good; Voltaire has no such illusions. Voltaire's version of the "noble savage" is one that is not noble, but brutal. Rousseau thought that Humankind's innate goodness was corrupted by civilization, including such things as private property.

**Why don't the Oreillons kill Candide and Cacambo?**

• Ever-practical Cacambo is able to keep the Oreillons from cooking and eating him and Candide. The Oreillons want to kill them because they think that Candide is a Jesuit. Cacambo convinces them that Candide is not a Jesuit, but has instead killed a Jesuit. From *Candide*:

> "But surely, gentlemen, you would not choose to eat your friends. You imagine you are going to roast a Jesuit, whereas my master is your friend, your defender, and you are going to spit the very man who has been destroying your enemies; as to myself, I am your countryman; this gentleman is my master, and so far from being a Jesuit, give me leave to tell you he has very lately killed one of that order, whose spoils he now wears, and which have probably occasioned your mistake. To convince you of the truth of what I say, take the habit he has on and carry it to the first barrier of the Jesuits' kingdom, and inquire whether my master did not kill one of their officers. There will be little or no time lost by this, and you may still reserve our bodies in your power to feast on if you should find what we have told you to be false. But, on the contrary, if you find it to be true, I am persuaded you are too well acquainted with the principles of the laws of society,

humanity, and justice, not to use us courteously, and suffer us to depart unhurt."

(Translation by Tobias Smollett)

# Chapter 17: "How Candide and his valet came to the land of Eldorado."

**Write travel directions to Eldorado. (Creative writing is allowed for this assignment.)**

- Some students may be creative in this assignment.

- In finding Eldorado, Candide and Cacambo abandon themselves to fate. They get on a boat and drift down a river. They go into a tunnel for 24 hours. When they come out of the tunnel, they are in a region that is surrounded by unscalable mountains.

- Eldorado is Eldorado in part because it is separate from the rest of the world. The bad things are kept out of Eldorado. (Compare the insane asylum in the satiric movie *King of Hearts*.)

- In Spanish, "Eldorado" means "the golden one."

- Lots of gold is in Eldorado, but it is not sought after by the citizens of Eldorado, although people outside Eldorado spent enormous efforts seeking gold. This is reminiscent of the Paradox of Happiness. If you pursue happiness, you will probably never find it. But if you direct your efforts to something satisfying that is not happiness, chances are that you will be happy (although, of course, all of us will experience some unhappiness during life).

- Candide and Cacambo have to undertake a dangerous journey in order to reach the utopia of Eldorado. This shows that Voltaire thought that utopias were almost impossible to reach. However, perhaps they are not impossible to achieve — or at least come close to achieving.

- Creative directions on how to reach Eldorado could include this step: Climb to the top of a rainbow, then turn right.

- Creative directions on how to reach Eldorado could include this step: Reform yourself.

**What do we learn about Eldorado in this chapter? (Also: What is Eldorado in myth?)**

• Eldorado is difficult — but not impossible — to get to. (Compare the garden of the final chapter.)

• Eldorado is wealthy, but its citizens seem to despise wealth — at least, the wealth of gold and precious jewels.

• Schools exist in Eldorado.

• Inns exist in Eldorado.

• The government is generous in Eldorado. Candide and Cacambo dine at an inn, and the government picks up the tab.

• Much food exists in Eldorado.

• By the way, the "red sheep" may be llamas.

• Many people believed that Eldorado actually existed in South America, and some explorers set out to find it.

• People work in Eldorado. As we find out in Chapter 30, work can actually be a blessing.

• Eldorado has a King. Men have power in Eldorado, although it is a much better society than we see elsewhere in *Candide*.

• Nowadays "Eldorado" simply means a utopia.

• These are some of Voltaire's sources for Eldorado:

> • Sir Walter Raleigh's *The Discoverie of the Large and Rich and Beautiful Empire of Guiana*, first published in 1595.

> • Sir Thomas More's *Utopia*, published in 1516.

> • Jonathan Swift's *Gulliver's Travels*, first published in 1726.

> • As a reminder, *Candide* was published in 1759.

# Chapter 18: "What they saw in the land of Eldorado."

**What do we learn about Eldorado in this chapter?**

• Few, if any, disagreements exist in Eldorado. All men are priests, and all men praise God.

• There is no Inquisition in Eldorado. There are no auto-da-fés in Eldorado.

• The citizens of Eldorado are not allowed to leave; however, Candide and Cacambo are permitted to leave — and the people of Eldorado spend a large sum of money in helping them to leave.

• In Eldorado is equality (even the King allows people to kiss him on both cheeks — and not his butt cheeks).

• Eldorado lacks churches and prisons. It lacks a Parliament and law courts. Eldorado does have science. From *Candide*:

> Candide asked to see the High Court of justice, the Parliament; but was answered that they had none in that country, being utter strangers to lawsuits. He then inquired if they had any prisons; they replied none. But what gave him at once the greatest surprise and pleasure was the Palace of Sciences, where he saw a gallery two thousand feet long, filled with the various apparatus in mathematics and natural philosophy.

(Translation by Tobias Smollett)

• Eldorado does have religion, but it is not an organized religion. From *Candide*:

> Cacambo asked in a respectful manner what was the established religion of El Dorado. The old man blushed

again and said, "Can there be two religions, then? Ours, I apprehend, is the religion of the whole world; we worship God from morning till night."

(Translation by Tobias Smollett)

• Eldorado is a utopia, and in it we have good things stressed. We see God's creation at its best, and we see human nature at its best.
• Critics of society can do two things. One is to criticize what is bad. Another is to point out what is good. (Roger Ebert was careful to point out both what was good and what was bad about a movie in his movie reviews.)
• One of the good things about Eldorado is the lack of religious intolerance.
• Another good thing about Eldorado is its prosperity. Everyone has enough. Although lots of gold and jewels are in Eldorado, they are used for building materials and decorative purposes rather than for money.
• Another good thing about Eldorado is a benevolent government. The government pays the bills for travelers.
• Another good thing about Eldorado is that it has schools and science. It also has work for everyone.
**Can we criticize Eldorado for anything?**
• Eldorado does have a lack of diversity. (Diversity is good as long as different people can live together in peace.)
• Eldorado is isolationist, although perhaps for good reason. If other people knew of the certain existence of Eldorado, they would invade it and carry off its gold and jewels. One of the good things about Eldorado is that it is so inaccessible. The United States of America has been blessed by the Atlantic Ocean and by the Pacific Ocean. The existence of these oceans historically made it more difficult to wage war on the United States.
• The people of Eldorado are not allowed to leave Eldorado.

• The people in Eldorado do not attempt to help people outside Eldorado. Presumably, the gold and jewels of Eldorado could be used to help other people.

• Eldorado corrupts Candide, although it is not the fault of Eldorado. Candide knows that the gold and jewels will make him rich in the outside world, and he becomes greedy enough that he wants to leave Eldorado. (Of course, he also wants to see Cunegonde again.)

• Eldoradoan society is in some ways unrealistic, I think. Law is one of the great inventions of Humankind, and I think that we ought to be grateful for the police and for courts of law.

• The old man is 172 years old. I doubt very much that anyone can live that long in the real world.

• Eldorado has a King. Men have power in Eldorado, although it is a much better society than we see elsewhere in *Candide*. A modern utopia would likely have men and women sharing power.

**Write a brief character analysis of the old man of Eldorado.**

• The old man is 172 years old. He is living a long and a happy life.

• The old man says that Eldorado is the former land of the Incas; the Incas left it in order to engage in conquest and were themselves conquered.

• The wise people stayed in Eldorado; they did not leave it.

• The old man knows much.

• He explains that in Eldorado all men are priests. Their sole ritual consists of thanking God.

**Write a brief character analysis of the King of Eldorado.**

• The citizens of Eldorado are not allowed to leave; however, Candide and Cacambo are permitted to leave — and the people of Eldorado spend large sums of money in helping them to leave.

• In Eldorado is equality (even the King of Eldorado allows people to kiss him on both cheeks — and not his butt cheeks). From *Candide*:

When they drew near to the presence-chamber, Cacambo asked one of the officers in what manner they were to pay their obeisance to His Majesty; whether it was the custom to fall upon their knees, or to prostrate themselves upon the ground; whether they were to put their hands upon their heads, or behind their backs; whether they were to lick the dust off the floor; in short, what was the ceremony usual on such occasions.

"The custom," said the great officer, "is to embrace the King and kiss him on each cheek."

(Translation by Tobias Smollett)

• The King does not understand why Candide and Cacambo wish to leave Eldorado.
• The King does not understand why Candide and Cacambo value gold and jewels so highly. By the way, the Europeans really did value gold highly. Hernán Cortez once said, "We Spanish suffer from a disease of the heart which can be cured only by gold." (Source: Sean Dolan, *Juan Ponce de Leon*, p. 60.)
**Why do Candide and Cacambo decide to leave Eldorado? Are their reasons good?**
• Candide wants to leave in part because Cunegonde is not there. That may be a good reason.
• Candide also wants to leave because he wants to be better than other people. In Eldorado, he will be equal to others, but outside of Eldorado (and armed with wealth from Eldorado), he can buy a kingdom and be a King. This is a bad reason.
• From *Candide*:

They spent a whole month in this hospitable place, during which time Candide was continually saying to Cacambo, "I own, my friend, once more, that the castle where I was born is a mere nothing in comparison to the place where we now are; but still Miss Cunegund is not here, and you yourself have doubtless some fair one in Europe for whom you sigh. If we remain here we shall only be as others are; whereas if we return to our own world with only a dozen of El Dorado sheep, loaded with the pebbles of this country, we shall be richer than all the kings in Europe; we shall no longer need to stand in awe of the Inquisitors; and we may easily recover Miss Cunegund."

This speech was perfectly agreeable to Cacambo. A fondness for roving, for making a figure in their own country, and for boasting of what they had seen in their travels, was so powerful in our two wanderers that they resolved to be no longer happy; and demanded permission of the King to quit the country.

(Translation by Tobias Smollett)

• Note that Cacambo agrees — unwisely — with Candide. Both of them like to travel.

• The scientists of Eldorado are able to construct a machine for conveying Candide and Cacambo and their new wealth over the mountains surrounding Eldorado.

**The religion of Eldorado can be understood as a form of Deism. What is Deism?**

• According to Deism, God created the universe, but God is not no longer involved in its day-to-day workings. This means that praying for a miracle won't work because God no longer performs miracles.

• Deism means that we need to help ourselves. If justice is going to be in the world, we ourselves have to bring justice into the world.

• According to Deism, the universe obeys natural laws that can be discovered through science.

• With Deism, we need not have churches and organized religion. We don't need to ask God for things because God does not answer prayers. The people of Eldorado simply thank God; they don't ask God for more possessions.

• Since God's laws can be discovered through science, we don't need to fight wars in order to resolve disputes about what God's laws are.

# Chapter 19: "What happened to them at Surinam, and how Candide became acquainted with Martin."

**Describe the life of the slave in Chapter 19.**

- Candide and Cacambo reach so-called "civilization," and they quickly see again the evil that exists in the real world. They see a slave.
- This slave is not wearing much clothing. He is wearing only half of a habit.
- The slave was sold by his mother.
- The slave, who is black, has only one hand and only one leg. The slave got his finger caught in a sugar mill, and so his hand was cut off — cutting the slave's hand off allows the mill to keep running, thus making money for the white owners of the slave. When the slave tried to run away, he was caught and his leg was cut off. From *Candide*:

> "Yes, sir," said the Negro; "it is the custom here. They give a linen garment twice a year, and that is all our covering. When we labor in the sugar works, and the mill happens to snatch hold of a finger, they instantly chop off our hand; and when we attempt to run away, they cut off a leg. Both these cases have happened to me, and it is at this expense that you eat sugar in Europe; and yet when my mother sold me for ten patacoons on the coast of Guinea, she said to me, 'My dear child, bless our fetishes; adore them forever; they will make thee live happy; thou hast the honor to be a slave to our lords the whites, by which thou wilt make the fortune of us thy parents.'"

> (Translation by Tobias Smollett)

• Voltaire is a satirist, and satire is humorous criticism. Voltaire is able to find humor even in cannibalism, as when he writes about how the old woman loses one buttock. However, Voltaire is NOT able to find any humor in the life of the slave. Some evils are so great that they can defeat satire.

• Nevertheless, Voltaire criticizes evil here, although it is not humorous criticism. Once again, what Christians say and what Christians do can be very different things. From *Candide*:

> "Alas! I know not whether I have made their fortunes; but they have not made mine; dogs, monkeys, and parrots are a thousand times less wretched than I. The Dutch fetishes who converted me tell me every Sunday that the blacks and whites are all children of one father, whom they call Adam. As for me, I do not understand anything of genealogies; but if what these preachers say is true, we are all second cousins; and you must allow that it is impossible to be worse treated by our relations than we are."

> (Translation by Tobias Smollett)

• One result of Candide's meeting with the slave is that he renounces optimism and becomes a pessimist. From *Candide*:

> "O Pangloss!" cried out Candide, "such horrid doings never entered thy imagination. Here is an end of the matter. I find myself, after all, obliged to renounce thy Optimism."

> "Optimism," said Cacambo, "what is that?"

> "Alas!" replied Candide, "it is the obstinacy of maintaining that everything is best when it is worst."

> (Translation by Tobias Smollett)

• Candide and Cacambo meet the slave in Dutch Guiana.

• Many people hoped that the New World of the Americas would be a better world than the Old World. However, this chapter shows that the New World has been corrupted by the Old World.

**In this chapter, we see some of the evils of slavery. If you feel like doing research, investigate and describe some of the evils of slavery in America, including in the United States before the Civil War.**

• The Europeans really did treat slaves badly. Many of the slaves were Native Americans. All of the Native Americans were liable to be forced to labor for the Europeans and/or forced to bring them tribute. On the island that now is the nations of the Dominican Republic and Haiti, Christopher Columbus forced Native Americans to bring him gold. Those who did not had their hands cut off. Most of them bled to death. The Spanish conquistadors committed many, many atrocities in the New World. (Source: Sean Dolan, *Juan Ponce de Leon*, p. 64.)

• Things that are very good can be used for things that are very evil. For example, during the Middle Passage across the Atlantic Ocean the crews of slave ships would bring slaves up on deck to dance. This practice was known as "dancing the slaves." The captains of the slave ships believed that the dancing would keep the slaves looking healthy so that they could be sold for a high price. Sometimes, the slaves were forced to sing as they danced. As you would expect, the songs were mournful laments about being forced into exile. (Source: Angela Shelf Medearis, and Michael R. Medearis, *Dance*, pp. 10-13.)

• In the days of slavery, African-Americans had few ways of helping each other. Baumfree, a slave in Hurley, New York, discovered that Isabella, his young daughter, had become the property of a harsh master named John Nealy who beat her. Once, he had beaten her with a hot rod and scarred her for life. As a slave, Baumfree was unable to get protection for her from the law courts. However, he did what he could do. He found another slave owner who did not beat his slaves, and he convinced him to buy his daughter. Later, as a free woman, Isabella became famous as an abolitionist and women's rights activist under the name Sojourner Truth. (Source: Catherine Bernard, *Sojourner Truth: Abolitionist and Women's Rights Activist*, pp. 18-19.)

• In the days of slavery, a slave mother would sometimes be separated from her children. On a small farm in Tennessee, a slave named Fanny had an infant. Fanny's owner wanted to separate Fanny from her infant. Fanny picked up the infant and threatened to bash its brains out unless her master allowed her to take her baby with her. Her master relented, and Fanny took the infant with her. In another, much less happy story, a slave woman named Margaret Garner tried to escape and run to freedom, taking her children with her. She was recaptured, but she succeeded in killing two of her children first, preferring that they die rather than be returned to slavery. (Source: Martha E. Kendall, *Failure is Impossible! The History of American Women's Rights*, pp. 33-34.)

• As a child, Harriet Tubman was a slave who was beaten often because of her independent nature. She quickly learned to wear extra clothing as padding and to cry and scream as if the blows hurt her. In 1849, she escaped from her owners and gained her freedom in the North, where she became a conductor for the Underground Railroad, guiding escaped slaves from one station to another. This was dangerous work, as she might have been killed if Southerners had caught her helping escaped slaves, but her motto as conductor was, "I can't die but once." (Source: Linda Jacob Altman, *Slavery and Abolition in American History*, p. 66.)

**Has Candide changed? Compare the Candide of Chapter 19 to the Candide of Chapter 5.**

• We see two main changes in Candide:

1. Early in this short novel, Candide was not materialistic. However, he was willing to leave Eldorado in part because he knew that he would be rich outside of Eldorado as long as he

had some of the gold and the jewels of Eldorado. Of course, he also wanted to see Cunegonde again.

2. Now, Candide is not merely puzzled by the way that his real-world experiences contradict Dr. Pangloss' philosophical optimism. Now, after seeing the slave, Candide actively denounces philosophical optimism.

**Why do Cacambo and Candide split up?**
• We find out that Cunegonde is now the favorite mistress of the Governor in Buenos Aires.
• Cacambo and Candide split up. Cacambo is to go to Buenos Aires and buy Cunegonde. Candide is to go to Venice and wait for Cacambo and Cunegonde to come to him. From *Candide*:

> "Oh, ho!" said the shipmaster, "if that is the case, get whom you please to carry you to Buenos Ayres; for my part, I wash my hands of the affair. It would prove a hanging matter to us all. The fair Cunegund is the Governor's favorite mistress."

> These words were like a clap of thunder to Candide; he wept bitterly for a long time, and, taking Cacambo aside, he said to him, "I'll tell you, my dear friend, what you must do. We have each of us in our pockets to the value of five or six millions in diamonds; you are cleverer at these matters than I; you must go to Buenos Ayres and bring off Miss Cunegund. If the Governor makes any difficulty give him a million; if he holds out, give him two; as you have not killed an Inquisitor, they will have no suspicion of you. I'll fit out another ship and go to Venice, where I will wait for you. Venice is a free country, where we shall have nothing to fear from Bulgarians, Abares, Jews or Inquisitors."

Cacambo greatly applauded this wise resolution. He was inconsolable at the thoughts of parting with so good a master, who treated him more like an intimate friend than a servant; but the pleasure of being able to do him a service soon got the better of his sorrow. They embraced each other with a flood of tears. Candide charged him not to forget the old woman. Cacambo set out the same day. This Cacambo was a very honest fellow.

(Translation by Tobias Smollett)

# Chapter 20: "What happened to Candide and Martin at sea."

**Write a brief character analysis of Mynheer Vanderdendur. (Compare and contrast him to James the Anabaptist.)**

- We can compare and contrast the Dutch merchant Mynheer Vanderdendur with another Dutch merchant: the Anabaptist Jacques.

- Both are Dutch merchants.

- Mynheer Vanderdendur is evil and rips off Candide, while the Anabaptist Jacques is kind and helps Candide.

- Mynheer Vanderdendur drowns while trying to rob a ship, and the Anabaptist Jacques drowns because he tried to save the life of another person.

**Write a brief character analysis of Martin, based on what you learn about him in these chapters. (Martin can be regarded as a foil to Dr. Pangloss.)**

- Here are a couple of definitions of "foil":

A character that serves by contrast to highlight or emphasize opposing traits in another character. For instance, in the film *Chasing Amy*, the character Silent Bob is a foil for his partner, Jake [sic; should be "Jay"], who is loquacious and foul-mouthed. In Shakespeare's *Hamlet*, Laertes the man of action is a foil to the reluctant Hamlet. The angry hothead Hotspur in *Henry IV, Part I,* is the foil to the cool and calculating Prince Hal.

Source: http://guweb2.gonzaga.edu/faculty/wheeler/lit_terms_F.html

A foil is a character whose personality and attitude is opposite the personality and attitude of another character.

Because these characters contrast, each makes the personality of the other stand out. In Sophocles' *Antigone*, Ismene is a foil for Antigone. Where Antigone is aware of the world, Ismene denies knowledge and hides from it. Where Antigone stands up to authority, Ismene withers before it. Antigone is active and Ismene is passive. Ismene's presence in the play highlights the qualities Antigone will display in her conflict with Creon making her an excellent foil.

Source: http://masconomet.org/teachers/trevenen/litterms.htm#F

• Candide has a number of advisors:

  • Dr. Pangloss: a philosophical optimist.
  • Martin: a pessimist.
  • Cacambo: a practical advisor.
  • The old woman: a practical advisor.

• Candide holds a contest to see who is the most miserable person in the area. He will choose one person to be his companion on his voyage back to the Old World. From *Candide*:

At length he determined in favor of a poor scholar, who had labored ten years for the booksellers at Amsterdam: being of opinion that no employment could be more detestable.

This scholar, who was in fact a very honest man, had been robbed by his wife, beaten by his son, and forsaken by his daughter, who had run away with a Portuguese. He had been likewise deprived of a small employment on which he subsisted, and he was persecuted by the clergy of Surinam, who took him for a Socinian. It must be acknowledged that the other competitors were, at least, as wretched as he; but Candide was in hopes that the company of a man of letters would relieve the tediousness of the voyage. All the other candidates complained that Candide had done them great injustice, but he stopped their mouths by a present of a hundred piastres to each.

(Translation by Tobias Smollett)

• Like other people in *Candide*, Martin is a victim of religious intolerance. People think that he is a Socinian, a member of a sect that denied the Trinity and the divinity of Christ, among other Christian tenets.

• Martin is the final major character of *Candide*. He is a total pessimist and cynic. From *Candide*:

> "And yet there is some good in the world," replied Candide.
> "Maybe so," said Martin, "but it has escaped my knowledge."
> (Translation by Tobias Smollett)

**Martin says that he is a Manichean. What is Manicheanism? However, Martin has been persecuted as a Socinian. What is Socinianism?**

*Manicheanism*

• Martin is a Manichean, although he is falsely accused of being a Socinian.

• The Manicheans are dualists. They see good and evil forces in the universe.

• Manicheans believe that the forces of good and of evil are eternally opposed and are equally powerful.

• Manicheans do not believe what Christians believe. Christians believe that God is more powerful than Satan. Manicheans would say that God is not omnipotent; instead, God and Satan are equally powerful.

- Manicheans can explain the presence of evil in the universe.
- Manicheanism is rejected by Christians as a heresy.
- Martin suffers religious persecution. Here he is persecuted as a Socinian, but his persecutors are mistaken. Martin is a Manichaean, not a Socinian.

*Socinianism*

- The Socinians rejected the doctrine of the Trinity and the divinity of Christ.
- The Socinians were a religious group that formed during the Reformation.
- The Unitarian Universalist church is influenced by the Socinians.
- We read this in a note at the end of the translation by Lowell Blair.

> Socinianism was a religious doctrine, condemned by the Inquisition in 1559, which denied a number of orthodox tenets, such as the divinity of Christ, the Trinity, and eternal punishment. (121)

**Candide says in Chapter 20 that "crime is sometimes punished" (Bair 79). Why? How does Martin respond? Who is right in this debate?**

- A battle occurs at sea between two ships. The Dutch pirate Vanderdendur's ship sinks. The Dutch pirate Vanderdendur is a scoundrel, and when he dies at sea, Candide says that sometimes vice/crime is punished.
- Martin replies that many people other than the Dutch pirate Vanderdendur also died when the pirate's ship sank.
- From *Candide*:

"You see," said Candide to Martin, "that vice is sometimes punished. This villain, the Dutch skipper, has met with the fate he deserved."

"Very true," said Martin, "but why should the passengers be doomed also to destruction? God has punished the knave, and the Devil has drowned the rest."

(Translation by Tobias Smollett)

### Is Martin's pessimism justified?

• I myself take a middle position — like Voltaire does, in my opinion. Good exists, and evil exists. I am not an optimist, nor am I a pessimist. To me, this is the realist position.

• Pangloss' optimism is simply wrong, and it can lead to quietism: the idea that we ought to do nothing. After all, if this is already the best of all possible worlds, why should we try to make it better?

• Martin's excessive pessimism can also lead to quietism. If everything is garbage, and whatever we do will not change that, then why should we try to do anything?

• Voltaire's middle position, I think, is correct. Evil exists, but we ought to fight evil.

• To me, Martin's excessive pessimism is more justifiable than Pangloss' excessive optimism, but a middle position is best.

# Chapter 21: "How Candide and Martin reasoned with each other as they approached the coast of France."

**What is Martin's view of Humankind, and for what reason does Martin think that the earth was created?**

- Martin thinks that the earth was created to drive us mad.
- Martin's view of Humankind is like his other views: pessimistic.
- Martin believes that Humankind has always been evil. Hawks have not changed their nature through the ages, so why would anyone think that humans have changed their nature?
- From *Candide*:

"But then, to what end," said Candide, "was the world formed?"

"To make us mad," said Martin.

(Translation by Tobias Smollett)

"Do you think," said Candide, "that mankind always massacred one another as they do now? Were they always guilty of lies, fraud, treachery, ingratitude, inconstancy, envy, ambition, and cruelty? Were they always thieves, fools, cowards, gluttons, drunkards, misers, calumniators, debauchees, fanatics, and hypocrites?"

"Do you believe," said Martin, "that hawks have always been accustomed to eat pigeons when they came in their way?"

"Doubtless," said Candide.

"Well then," replied Martin, "if hawks have always had the same nature, why should you pretend that mankind change theirs?"

"Oh," said Candide, "there is a great deal of difference; for free will — " and reasoning thus they arrived at Bordeaux.

(Translation by Tobias Smollett)

**Compare and contrast Dr. Pangloss and Martin. They are foils to each other.**

• Dr. Pangloss and Martin are foils to each other. Dr. Pangloss is relentlessly optimistic, while Martin is relentlessly pessimistic.

# Chapter 22: "What happened to Candide and Martin in France."

**Voltaire criticizes French and Parisian ways in this chapter. How does he do that?**

- Martin was robbed in Paris. In both Paris and the provinces, he found the people to be without sense.

- From *Candide*:

At length they descried the coast of France, when Candide said to Martin, "Pray, Monsieur Martin, were you ever in France?"

"Yes, sir," said Martin, "I have been in several provinces of that kingdom. In some, one half of the people are fools and madmen; in some, they are too artful; in others, again, they are, in general, either very good-natured or very brutal; while in others, they affect to be witty, and in all, their ruling passion is love, the next is slander, and the last is to talk nonsense."

"But, pray, Monsieur Martin, were you ever in Paris?"

"Yes, sir, I have been in that city, and it is a place that contains the several species just described; it is a chaos, a confused multitude, where everyone seeks for pleasure without being able to find it; at least, as far as I have observed during my short stay in that city. At my arrival I was robbed of all I had in the world by pickpockets and sharpers, at the fair of Saint-Germain. I was taken up myself for a robber, and confined in prison a whole week; after which I hired myself as corrector to a press in order to get a little money towards defraying my expenses back to Holland on foot. I knew the whole tribe of scribblers, malcontents, and fanatics. It is said the people of that city are very polite; I believe they may be."

(Translation by Tobias Smollett)

• Paris and Eldorado are foils. The two biggest sections of this short novel are the sections that are set in Eldorado and in Paris.

• Eldorado is filled with good people, but Paris is filled with evil people. As usual, Candide will be ripped off when he is Paris. The one place that Candide is not ripped is when he is in Eldorado.

**Explain who was Descartes, and what are Jansenism and Molinism.**

*Descartes*

Descartes is an important modern philosopher. He was a dualist, believing in both mind and body. In 1637, he published his *Discourse on Method*. A famous quotation by Descartes is "I think, therefore I am."

*Jansenism*

Jansenists believed in predestination. They advocated a return to holiness. Jansenism was a Roman Catholic Church movement. Cornelis Jansen (1585–1638), a Dutch Roman Catholic theologian, founded Jansenism. According to *The Columbia Encyclopedia*, Sixth Edition, 2001,

> Jansenism was strictly a Roman Catholic movement, and it had no repercussions in the Protestant world. Its fundamental purpose was a return of people to greater personal holiness, hence the characteristically mystical turn of Jansenist writings. St. Augustine's teaching on grace was especially appealing to Jansen, who stressed the doctrine that the soul must be converted to God by the action of divine

grace, without which conversion could not begin. Predestination was accepted in an extreme form and was so essential to Jansenism that its adherents were even referred to as Calvinists by their opponents. But Jansenism had no appeal to Protestants, for it held the necessity of the Roman Catholic Church for salvation and opposed justification by faith alone.

Jansenism, however, came into conflict with the church for its predestinarianism, for its discouragement of frequent communion for the faithful, and for its attack on the Jesuits and the new casuistry, which the Jansenists thought was demoralizing the confessional. Jansenism took root in France, especially among the clergy. There it early became involved with Gallicanism, and high officials of church and state often sided with Jansenists to thwart the Holy See.

Source:

http://www.bartleby.com/65/ja/Jansen-C.html

Date Downloaded: 26 December 2009

*Molinism*

Molinists believed in free will. They also believed in a philosophy known as quietism. According to *The Columbia Encyclopedia*, Sixth Edition, 2001,

"The essence of quietism is that perfection lies in the complete passivity of the soul before God and the absorption of the individual in the divine love to the point of annihilation not only of will but of all effort or desire for effort."

Source:



Date Downloaded: 2004.

This is quietism in the Christian faith. Another form of quietism is calm acceptance of the world as it is with no attempt to change it.

Molinism is another name for quietism. Miguel de Molinos, a 17th-century Spanish priest, founded Molinism. In 1687, Pope Innocent XI condemned Molinism as a heresy.

Here is a definition of Quietism from the Free Dictionary:

a heretical form of religious mysticism founded by Miguel de Molinos, a 17th-century Spanish priest. Molinism, or quietism, developed within the Roman Catholic Church in Spain and spread especially to France, where its most influential exponent was Madame Guyon. She preached her doctrines to members of the French aristocracy, winning a convert and friend in Madame de Maintenon, Louis XIV's wife, and an ally in Archbishop Fénelon. Another quietist was Antoinette Bourignon. The essence of quietism is that perfection lies in the complete passivity of the soul before God and the absorption of the individual in the divine love to the point of annihilation not only of will but of all effort or desire for effort. Molinos talked about an entire cessation of self-consciousness, and Madame Guyon maintained that she could not sin, for sin was self, and she had rid herself of self. Molinos and his doctrines were condemned by Pope Innocent XI in 1687. A commission in France found most of Madame Guyon's works intolerable, and in 1699 Pope Innocent XII prohibited the circulation of Fénelon's book, the *Maxims of the Saints*.

**Write a brief analysis of the medical practices that Candide undergoes and of the "friends" that he makes when he is ill.**

- In Paris, "friends" who want to take advantage of Candide surround him. Previously, when Martin was ill in Paris, he was poor and so he had no "friends" to "take care" of him.
- Candide's "friends" include:

1) "two doctors he had not sent for" (82)

2) "several intimate friends who would not leave him" (82)

3) "two pious and charitable ladies who kept him supplied with hot broth" (82)

- Of course, Candide is not really ill; he is merely tired from travelling.
- The bloodletting of the doctors, however, does make Candide really ill.
- "Phlebotomy " is the fancy name for bloodletting.
- George Washington, the first President of the United States, is thought to have died because of excessive blood-letting.
- Here is some information about phlebotomy:

**Phlebotomy: The Ancient Art of Bloodletting**

By Graham Ford

The practice of bloodletting seemed logical when the foundation of all medical treatment was based on the four body humors: blood, phlegm, yellow bile, and black bile. Health was thought to be restored by purging, starving, vomiting or bloodletting.

The art of bloodletting was flourishing well before Hippocrates in the fifth century B.C. By the middle ages, both surgeons and barbers were specializing in this bloody practice. Barbers advertised with a red (for blood) and white (for tourniquet) striped pole. The pole itself represented the stick squeezed by the patient to dilate the veins. [...]

Blood was caught in shallow bowls. During the 17th to 19th centuries, blood was also captured in small flint glass cups. Heated air inside the cups created a vacuum causing blood to flow into the cup — a handy technique for drawing blood from a localized area. This practice was called cupping.

Source:

http://www.mtn.org/quack/devices/phlebo.htm

Date Downloaded: 24 June 2004

**Write a brief character analysis of the little abbé from Périgord. What is an abbé?**
• "Abbé" is a title of respect that is given to Catholic priests or other clerics in France.
• The abbé is another person who takes advantage of Candide.
• The abbé is a parasite who attaches himself to people to see what he can get out of them. He is very willing to provide what they want as long as he gets something out of it.
• The abbé gets Candide to indulge in vices. For example, Candide loses a great deal of money playing cards — of course, the abbé gets a cut of Candide's losses (although Candide is unaware of it).

• After hearing about Cunegonde from Candide, the abbé decides to take advantage of him. Candide supposedly receives a letter from Cunegonde, and he goes to see her. (Candide has never received a letter from Cunegonde, so he does not know what her handwriting looks like.) However, he is unable to see her or to hear her voice (because of her "illness"); of course, Cunegonde is an imposter. Candide gives her a lot of wealth, which she and the abbé split.

• The best word to describe the abbé is "parasite," although the words "cheat," "swindler," "flatterer," and "hypocrite" also apply. A parasite is a person who lives off others.

**Write a brief character analysis of the marquise. (What is a "marquise"?)**

• The marquise has a daughter, whom she has taught to look for cheaters at cards. For example, the two look for cheaters who dog-ear their cards, meaning that they want to let their winnings ride — although they haven't won.

• She is out for what she can get. She praises a couple of diamonds on Candide's hand, so he gives them to her. (By the way, some people really are generous. Comedian Lou Costello was once visited by a friend, who had a drink of Scotch and praised it. When the friend went to his car, he discovered that Mr. Costello had placed a case of the Scotch he had praised in it. The friend was not a parasite — he quickly learned not to praise something when he was around Mr. Costello.)

• She is a lady of easy virtue. She seduces Candide, making him feel guilty for cheating on Cunegonde.

• A marquise is married to a marquis; another name for a marquise is "marchioness."

**Write a short character analysis of the scholar.**

• The scholar is very critical of tragedies. From *Candide*:

There was at the table a person of learning and taste, who supported what the Marchioness had advanced. They next began to talk of tragedies. The lady desired to know how it came about that there were several tragedies, which still continued to be played, though they would not bear reading? The man of taste explained very clearly how a piece may be in some manner interesting without having a grain of merit. He showed, in a few words, that it is not sufficient to throw together a few incidents that are to be met with in every romance, and that to dazzle the spectator the thoughts should be new, without being farfetched; frequently sublime, but always natural; the author should have a thorough knowledge of the human heart and make it speak properly; he should be a complete poet, without showing an affectation of it in any of the characters of his piece; he should be a perfect master of his language, speak it with all its purity, and with the utmost harmony, and yet so as not to make the sense a slave to the rhyme.

"Whoever," added he, "neglects any one of these rules, though he may write two or three tragedies with tolerable success, will never be reckoned in the number of good authors. There are very few good tragedies; some are idylls, in very well-written and harmonious dialogue; and others a chain of political reasonings that set one asleep, or else pompous and high-flown amplification, that disgust rather than please. Others again are the ravings of a madman, in an uncouth style, unmeaning flights, or long apostrophes to the deities, for want of knowing how to address mankind; in a word a collection of false maxims and dull commonplace."

(Translation by Tobias Smollett)

• The scholar is overcritical of great works of literature. He doesn't even like Homer's *Iliad*!

- The scholar himself is an unsuccessful writer. From *Candide*:

Candide listened to this discourse with great attention, and conceived a high opinion of the person who delivered it; and as the Marchioness had taken care to place him near her side, he took the liberty to whisper her softly in the ear and ask who this person was that spoke so well.

"He is a man of letters," replied Her Ladyship, "who never plays, and whom the abbé brings with him to my house sometimes to spend an evening. He is a great judge of writing, especially in tragedy; he has composed one himself, which was damned, and has written a book that was never seen out of his bookseller's shop, excepting only one copy, which he sent me with a dedication, to which he had prefixed my name."

(Translation by Tobias Smollett)

**Write a brief character analysis of the officer of the watch.**
- The officer of the watch is corrupt.
- Of course, "Cunegonde" is not really Cunegonde. Instead, the abbé has substituted an imposter to pose as Cunegonde, in order to get money from Candide.
- When "Cunegonde" has gotten the money, the abbé brings in an officer of the watch to arrest Candide. Martin recognizes what is happening, and he knows that the officer can be bribed to let Candide go. That is what Candide does.
- An attempt has been made to kill Louis XIV, King of France from 1638-1715. Because of this, foreigners such as Candide and Martin are under suspicion.

**How does Voltaire criticize Parisian society in this chapter?**
- We have a lot of criticism of Paris in this chapter.

• Nearly everyone whom Candide meets is trying to take advantage of him. He has wealth, and so he has lots of "friends."

• The abbé is certainly evil. He is a "guide" for Candide, but of course what he is after is money for himself. He takes Candide to a card game, and he gets a cut of the money that Candide loses in the card game.

• One thing we see in this chapter is a discussion of literature. The scholar is certainly overcritical of great works of literature. He doesn't even like Homer's *Iliad*!

**What does Martin do in this chapter?**

• Martin is not surprised when Candide never has any aces when he is gambling.

• Martin is a guide, an advisor, and a philosophical commentator in this short novel.

• Martin remains a Manichean in this chapter.

• Martin does not do much to protect Candide in this chapter. He does not advise Candide not to gamble. Apparently, Martin is such a pessimist that he figures that if Candide does not lose his money gambling, he will lose it in some other way. Martin is right.

• Martin is aware that the Officer of the Watch can be bribed. He does keep Candide and himself out of jail by telling Candide that the Officer of the Watch can be bribed.

# Chapter 23: "How Candide and Martin reached the coast of England, and what they saw there."

**If you feel like doing research, explain the death of Admiral John Byng, who after being defeated by La Galissonniere, was executed in 1757.**

• In 1756, Admiral John Byng was ordered to relieve the island of Minorca when it was under attack. He did give the order to engage the enemy's fleet, but unfortunately the van suffered heavy losses. Admiral Byng's own ships were in the rear, but through mishaps, they barely got within firing range of the enemy's ships. After losing the battle, Admiral Byng sailed away, leaving the island of Minorca to the enemy. He was court-martialed, found guilty of neglect of duty, and sentenced to die. No pardon came from the King, and on March 14, 1757, Admiral Byng was executed by firing squad. Before being executed, he was asked if he wanted to wear a handkerchief over his face. He replied, "If my face will frighten them, let it be done. They will not frighten me."

• Voltaire is able even to make an execution by firing squad funny. Candide hears the reason for the execution, and he points out that the French admiral was as far from the English admiral as the English admiral was from the French admiral:

> "There is no doubt of that; but in this country it is found
> requisite, now and then, to put an admiral to death, in order
> to encourage the others to fight."

(Translation by Tobias Smollett)

• The war that Admiral John Byng was fighting in was the Seven Years' War. As a result of the war, Great Britain emerged as the leading colonial power in North America, while France ceased to be the leading colonial power in North America.

- The island of Majorca is in the Mediterranean.
- Martin says this about the war:

"You know that these two nations are at war about a few acres of barren land in the neighborhood of Canada, and that they have expended much greater sums in the contest than all Canada is worth. To say exactly whether there are a greater number fit to be inhabitants of a madhouse in the one country than the other, exceeds the limits of my imperfect capacity; I know in general that the people we are going to visit are of a very dark and gloomy disposition."

(Translation by Tobias Smollett)

# Chapter 24: "Paquette and Brother Giroflée."

**Write a brief character analysis of Paquette.**

- Paquette is one of the many characters in this short novel who disappear for a while and then show up again.

- When Candide first sees Paquette, he does not look closely at her and so does not recognize her, but he thinks that she is very happy. This, of course, turns out to be mistaken.

- Paquette is promiscuous. At the beginning of this short novel, she was having sex with Dr. Pangloss, and she gave him syphilis. We find out that a Franciscan, who was her confessor, seduced her.

- A doctor took pity on her and cured her of her sexually transmitted disease. She became his mistress. The doctor murdered his wife. Paquette was accused of the murder. A judge let her off, but she had to consent to be his mistress. Soon he grew tired of her. Now Paquette makes a very hard living as a prostitute.

- Paquette appeared to be happy when Candide saw her with the monk, Brother Giroflée, but she was not happy. Instead, appearing to be happy when one is not is simply part of the trade of being a prostitute.

- These days we read of higher-class prostitutes giving clients what they call a girlfriend experience. This is not Wham, Bam, Thank You, Ma'am. It takes more time than that and is more expensive. Apparently, Ashlee Dupree, the call girl who brought down a governor of New York, was someone who gave a girlfriend experience.

- Porn stars are like Paquette in that they really do act. They have sex on screen, and sometimes they don't feel like having sex. It is hard, however, to know the truth about female porn stars. Some female porn stars will tell interviewers what they think the interviewers want to hear. Some female porn stars go into porn with their eyes wide open.

• The main point, of course, is that Candide thought that Paquette was happy, but she turns out to be very unhappy.

• Paquette is a likable character. She seems more a victim than a victimizer. Of course, we are hearing only her side of the story.

• Paquette's story is similar to the old woman's. Both of them go (or went) from man to man. Both of them are victims.

• Of course, we see more satire of religion here. Many of the men whom Paquette has slept with are religious people, including her confessor. None of these people ought to be victimizing Paquette. Many of these religious people ought to be celibate.

• Other occupations come under Voltaire's satiric attack. A doctor takes advantage of Paquette. The doctor will cure her STD only if Paquette sleeps with him. A judge will find her innocent of murder only if she sleeps with him.

**Write a brief character analysis of Brother Giroflée.**

• Brother Giroflée is a monk who spends money on prostitutes such as Paquette.

• Brother Giroflée did not want to be a monk; he was forced to become a monk (and take a vow of poverty) at age 15 so that his parents could leave more of their property to another, older son.

• Once again, we see someone who is unhappy.

• Brother Giroflée says that the situation of the other monks is like his; they too are unhappy.

**At this point in the short novel, whose views seem to be more correct: Pangloss' or Martin's?**

• Pretty clearly, Martin's pessimism seems to be a more accurate description of the world than Dr. Pangloss' optimism. Pretty clearly, evil exists in this world.

# Chapter 25: "A visit to Signor Pococurante, Venetian nobleman."

**Write a brief character analysis of Signor Pococurante. What does the name "Pococurante" mean?**

• A note in the Bantam Classic edition containing the translation by Lowell Bair explains that "Pococurante" means "caring little" (122).

• Pococurante is overly critical. He is wealthy, and he has everything, but he does not appreciate it.

• Pococurante suffers from boredom. He gets no pleasure from life or from his possessions. He is wealthy, so he does not have to work.

• Pococurante expresses his own opinions — something that Candide was not raised to do. From *Candide*:

> Candide, who had been brought up with a notion of never making use of his own judgment, was astonished at what he heard; but Martin found there was a good deal of reason in the senator's remarks.

(Translation by Tobias Smollett)

• Most of us would disagree with Pococurante's negative assessments of great works of literature and of art.

**Why doesn't Pococurante care for all the good things he has? Why is he bored?**

Here are a few possible answers:

1) Pococurante has not had to work for what he has. If he had had to work for the things he has, he would appreciate them more. If he were to work, he would probably not suffer so much from boredom.

2) Pococurante is not himself creative. If he were a creator instead of merely a consumer, he would appreciate the great works of art he has. If he were a creator, he would probably not suffer so much from boredom.

Some types of work can be a blessing.
Creative work can be a blessing.

**In your opinion (which is not necessarily the opinion expressed in Chapter 25), is a life of criticism (of works of art) a worthy life?**

• In my opinion, a life of criticism is a worthy life. However, one must not be overly critical.

• Roger Ebert is a person who lived a life of criticism. (And of creation.) Mr. Ebert was not overly critical. He was careful to give praise where praise is deserved. Even if he gave thumbs down on a movie, if something about the movie deserved to be praised, he praised it. He was also willing to completely pan a movie if the movie deserved to be completely panned. One of his books is titled *Your Movie Sucks*. A photograph of a p*ssed-off Roger Ebert appears on the cover.

• Pococurante does not create.

• Criticism should help us to enjoy great works of art as well as to know why bad works of art are not good.

**Pococurante refers to many great authors and other creative notables. If you feel like doing research, explain who a few of these people are. (Avoid plagiarism.)**

*Lodovico Ariosto (1471-1533)*

This Italian Renaissance poet is the author of the comic epic *Orlando Furioso*.

*Marcus Tullius Cicero, aka Tully (106-43 B.C.E.)*

Roman orator, statesman, and author. He committed suicide after being marked for death by Mark Anthony.

*Homer (Ninth Century B.C.E.)*

Greek who was the author of the epic poems the *Iliad* and the *Odyssey*. The *Iliad* is about the wrath of Achilles during the Trojan War. At first, Achilles was angry at the Greek leader Agamemnon. Later, he directed his anger toward Hector, the leader of the Trojan troops. The *Odyssey* tells the story of what happened to Odysseus after the Fall of Troy. Odysseus wandered the Mediterranean for 10 years before returning to his home island, Ithaca. All of the warriors who sailed to Troy with him had died before Odysseus reached Ithaca, so he had to figure out how to get rid of over 100 suitors who thought he was dead and who were attempting to marry his wife, Penelope.

*Horace (65-8 B.C.E.)*

Roman poet who wrote *Odes*.

*John Milton (1608-1674)*

English poet and author of *Paradise Lost*.

*Raphael (1483-1520)*

Italian Renaissance architect and painter. Mark Twain once criticized a painting by Raphael, claiming that Raphael put too much weight in a boat that was incapable of carrying it.

*Seneca (4 B.C.E.?-65 C.E.)*

Roman philosopher and dramatist.

*Torquato Tasso (1544-1595)*

Italian epic poet of the late Renaissance. He wrote *Jerusalem Delivered*.

*Virgil (70-19 B.C.E.)*

Latin poet, and the author of the epic poem *Aeneid*. The *Aeneid* contains our fullest surviving account of the Fall of Troy. It tells about Troy's end and of how Aeneas fulfilled his duty to go to Italy and become an important ancestor of the Roman people.

# Chapter 26: "How Candide and Martin had supper with six foreigners, and who they were."

**Who are the six foreigners? If you feel like doing research, investigate and report the story of one or more of the foreigners.**

• The main satiric point here is that evil things happen to everybody, even to kings. Evil also happens to commoners, of course, and Candide discovers that Cacambo is now a slave. No one should feel safe because he or she is in a high position.

• These are the six kings, all of whom are real and historical people:

1) *Ahmed III.*

A great sultan. Dethroned his brother. His nephew dethroned him. He lived from 1673 to 1736, and he was deposed in 1730. From *Candide*:

> "I am not joking in the least, my name is Achmet III. I was Grand Sultan for many years; I dethroned my brother, my nephew dethroned me, my viziers lost their heads, and I am condemned to end my days in the old seraglio. My nephew, the Grand Sultan Mahomet, gives me permission to travel sometimes for my health, and I am come to spend the Carnival at Venice."

(Translation by Tobias Smollett)

Cacambo is now the slave of this deposed Sultan.

2) *Ivan, Emperor of all the Russias.*

Dethroned as an infant. Brought up in prison. Ivan VI was proclaimed emperor at months old in 1740. He was deposed in December 1741 and spent the rest of his life in prison until he was killed in 1764. From *Candide*:

"My name is Ivan. I was once Emperor of all the Russians, but was dethroned in my cradle. My parents were confined, and I was brought up in a prison, yet I am sometimes allowed to travel, though always with persons to keep a guard over me, and I come to spend the Carnival at Venice."

(Translation by Tobias Smollett)

3) *Charles Edward, King of England.*
His father ceded him the rights to the throne. Fought to maintain these rights. Put in prison. He is the Young Pretender, whose supporters called him Bonnie Prince Charles (1720-1788). From *Candide*:

"I am Charles Edward, King of England; my father has renounced his right to the throne in my favor. I have fought in defense of my rights, and near a thousand of my friends have had their hearts taken out of their bodies alive and thrown in their faces. I have myself been confined in a prison. I am going to Rome to visit the King, my father, who was dethroned as well as myself; and my grandfather and I have come to spend the Carnival at Venice."

(Translation by Tobias Smollett)

4) *King of Poland.*
War took away his hereditary dominions. He is King Augustus III (1696-1763). From *Candide*:

"I am the King of Poland; the fortune of war has stripped me of my hereditary dominions. My father experienced the same vicissitudes of fate. I resign myself to the will of Providence, in the same manner as Sultan Achmet, the

Emperor Ivan, and King Charles Edward, whom God long preserve; and I have come to spend the Carnival at Venice."

(Translation by Tobias Smollett)

5) *Another King of Poland.*
Lost his kingdom twice. He is Stanislas Leczinski (1677-1766). From *Candide*:

> "I am King of Poland also. I have twice lost my kingdom; but Providence has given me other dominions, where I have done more good than all the Sarmatian kings put together were ever able to do on the banks of the Vistula; I resign myself likewise to Providence; and have come to spend the Carnival at Venice."

(Translation by Tobias Smollett)

6) *Theodore, King of Corsica.*
Now penniless. He is Theodore von Neuhof (1690-1756). From *Candide*:

> "Gentlemen," said he, "I am not so great a prince as the rest of you, it is true, but I am, however, a crowned head. I am Theodore, elected King of Corsica. I have had the title of Majesty, and am now hardly treated with common civility. I have coined money, and am not now worth a single ducat. I have had two secretaries, and am now without a valet. I was once seated on a throne, and since that have lain upon a truss of straw, in a common jail in London, and I very much fear I shall meet with the same fate here in Venice, where I came, like Your Majesties, to divert myself at the Carnival."

(Translation by Tobias Smollett)

# Chapter 27: "Candide's voyage to Constantinople."

**What has happened to Cacambo and Cunegonde?**

*Cacambo*

Cacambo is now a slave to the Sultan, although Candide soon ransoms him.

Cacambo, of course, has no money left of all the riches that he had after leaving El Dorado. Much of the money went to buy Cunegonde's freedom, and a pirate robbed him of the rest and then sold him into slavery, along with Cunegonde.

*Cunegonde*

Cunegonde lost her freedom when Cacambo lost his money. She has grown horribly ugly, and she is a slave who works hard, washing dishes and doing other work. Even though she has grown horribly ugly, Candide wants to marry her.

**What has happened to Dr. Pangloss and the young Baron?**

Dr. Pangloss and the young Baron are slaves on the ship on which Candide, Cacambo, and Martin are sailing. Pangloss and the young Baron are helping to row the ship, and they are whipped often.

# Chapter 28: "What happened to Candide, Cunegonde, Pangloss, Martin, etc."

**What are the stories of Pangloss and the Baron?**

*The Young Baron*

• Of course, Candide had only wounded, not killed, the Baron, who was cured of the wound.

• Some Spanish troops attacked him and carried him off and put him in prison in Buenos Aires.

• The Baron was given permission to travel to Rome, where he was given the job of chaplain to the French Ambassador in Constantinople.

• The Baron's homosexuality surfaces when he bathes with a young Turk. A Christian and a Turk being naked together is against the law, and the Baron is whipped on the soles of his feet and then sent to be a slave in the galleys.

• When Candide ransoms the Baron, the Baron's pride surfaces. He merely nods to Candide and promises to pay him back as soon as possible.

• From *Candide*:

"I was a little too hasty I must own; but as you seem to be desirous to know by what accident I came to be a slave on board the galley where you saw me, I will inform you. After I had been cured of the wound you gave me, by the College apothecary, I was attacked and carried off by a party of Spanish troops, who clapped me in prison in Buenos Ayres, at the very time my sister was setting out from there. I asked leave to return to Rome, to the general of my Order, who appointed me chaplain to the French Ambassador at Constantinople. I had not been a week in my new office, when I happened to meet one evening a young Icoglan, extremely handsome and well-made. The weather was very hot; the young man had an inclination to bathe. I took the opportunity to bathe likewise. I did not know it was a crime for a Christian to be found naked in company with a young Turk. A cadi ordered me to receive a hundred blows on the soles of my feet, and sent me to the galleys. I do not believe that there was ever an act of more flagrant injustice. But I would fain know how my sister came to be a scullion to a Transylvanian prince, who has taken refuge among the Turks?"

(Translation by Tobias Smollett)

*Pangloss*

• Pangloss was hanged instead of being burned at the stake because the rain made it too difficult to start a fire.

• The hanging did not kill Pangloss, as a surgeon who bought Pangloss' body in order to dissect it discovered. The doctor started to dissect the body, and Pangloss regained consciousness. Fortunately, the doctor was able to restore him to health.

• Pangloss got a job with a merchant, who took him to Constantinople. There Pangloss' heterosexuality played a role in making him a slave. A young Muslim girl had a bouquet in her cleavage. The bouquet fell out of her cleavage, and Pangloss returned it there. He took so long in returning it that he was arrested, whipped on the soles of his feet, and then made a slave on a galley.

• When Candide buys Pangloss' freedom, Pangloss falls to his knees and thanks him profusely.

• Pangloss is still a philosophical optimist, and he still thinks that Leibniz is correct.

• From *Candide*:

"One day I happened to enter a mosque, where I saw no one but an old man and a very pretty young female devotee, who was telling her beads; her neck was quite bare, and in her bosom she had a beautiful nosegay of tulips, roses, anemones, ranunculuses, hyacinths, and auriculas; she let fall her nosegay. I ran immediately to take it up, and presented it to her with a most respectful bow. I was so long in delivering [the John Butt translation has "replaced it" (135); the translation by Lowell Bair has "put it back" (114)] it that the man began to be angry; and, perceiving I was a Christian, he cried out for help; they carried me before the cadi, who ordered me to receive one hundred bastinadoes, and sent me to the galleys. I was chained in the very galley and to the very same bench with the Baron. On board this galley there were four young men belonging to Marseilles, five Neapolitan priests, and two monks of Corfu, who told us that the like adventures happened every day. The Baron pretended that he had been worse used than myself; and I insisted that there was far less harm in taking up a nosegay, and putting it into a woman's bosom, than to be found stark naked with a young Icoglan. We were continually whipped, and received twenty lashes a day with a heavy thong, when the concatenation of sublunary events brought you on board our galley to ransom us from slavery."

(Translation by Tobias Smollett)

• This short novel is coming to an end, and we have lots of loose ends being tied up now. All of the major characters in the novel are being brought together.

# Chapter 29: "How Candide found Cunegonde and the old woman again."

**Is Candide an honorable man?**

• Yes, Candide always tries to do the right thing.

• Candide decides to marry (and honor his promise) to marry Cunegonde even though she is now ugly (like the old woman).

• Candide rescues Cacambo, Pangloss, and the young Baron. He also rescues Cunegonde and the old woman.

• Candide even buys a small farm for everyone to live on. He uses the last of his money to buy the small farm.

**Why doesn't the young Baron want Candide to marry Cunegonde, his sister?**

• The young Baron is still proud. He doesn't want Candide to marry his sister because Candide is not noble. This is the same reason he gave earlier in South America when Candide first told him that he wished to marry his sister.

**Has Candide changed thus far in the novel? (Compare how Candide treats the young Baron now to how he treated him in Chapter 15.)**

• In South America, when Candide got angry with the Baron for not wanting him to marry Cunegonde, Candide wounded the young Baron with a sword. Candide even thought that he had killed the young Baron. Now, Candide simply uses words, not his sword, against the young Baron.

• In South America, after stabbing the young Baron, Candide regretted his actions. Now, he scorns the young Baron.

• Candide now appears to be more mature. He does not react with violence when he is angry. He also appears more capable of making up his own mind. He knows that the young Baron is behaving wrongly and ungratefully, and Candide is angry because of this. Candide does not show deference to the young Baron because of his rank.

- From *Candide*:

"Thou foolish fellow," said Candide, "have I not delivered thee from the galleys, paid thy ransom, and thy sister's, too, who was a scullion, and is very ugly, and yet condescend to marry her? and shalt thou pretend to oppose the match! If I were to listen only to the dictates of my anger, I should kill thee again."

(Translation by Tobias Smollett)

# Chapter 30: "Conclusion."

**What happens to the young Baron?**

• Candide and most of his friends engage in some evil here. They make the young Baron a galley slave again.

• Of course, they do not tell Cunegonde what they have done.

• It can be good to get rid of the proud people in your life. Choose your friends wisely. Avoid evil and negative and proud people. (Don't make them galley slaves.)

**Are Candide and the others happy on the small farm?**

No, they are not happy:

*Cunegonde*

She becomes uglier and uglier, and she has a disagreeable personality.

*The Old Woman*

The old woman becomes feeble and is always in a foul mood.

*Cacambo*

Cacambo works hard, but his work exhausts him, and he is miserable.

*Pangloss*

Pangloss is unhappy because he is not a professor at a German university. Many people despair and give up when their careers don't go the way they want them to go, and Pangloss is one of them.

*Martin*

One advantage of being a pessimist is that you are not surprised when things work out badly. Martin bears everything patiently.

**What has happened to Paquette and Brother Giroflée?**

• Paquette and Brother Giroflée arrive at the little farm one day. They are poverty stricken.

• They have quarreled and reconciled. They have been in prison.

• Brother Giroflée has become a Turk (Moslem).

• Paquette is still a prostitute, but her trade earns her no money.

**How does the "best philosopher" — a dervish — in Turkey treat Candide and his friends? (What is a dervish?)**

• Badly. He ends up slamming the door in their faces. (However, he does say things that —interpreted correctly — are in my opinion sensible.)

• Candide and the others basically want to know the meaning of life. They also want to know about evil. The dervish apparently has no interest in those questions — and apparently has no answers.

• Or the dervish may be saying that such philosophizing is worthless. We are here, and evil is here. These are facts, and we must deal with them. Taking action is worth more than philosophizing.

• The dervish may be saying that this is the world we have to live in. Deal with it.

• The dervish does give some advice: "Be silent" (translation by Tobias Smollett). In other words, don't philosophize. Or perhaps: Don't engage in bad kinds of philosophizing.

• Here is a definition of "dervish":

1. A member of any of various Muslim ascetic orders, some of which perform whirling dances and vigorous chanting as acts of ecstatic devotion.

2. One that possesses abundant, often frenzied energy: "[She] is a dervish of unfocused energy, an accident about to happen" (Jane Gross).

ETYMOLOGY: Turkish dervi, mendicant, from Persian darvsh.

WORD HISTORY: The word "dervish" calls to mind the phrases "howling dervish" and "whirling dervish." Certainly there are dervishes whose religious exercises include making loud howling noises or whirling rapidly to induce a dizzy, mystical state. But a dervish is really the Muslim equivalent of a monk or friar, for the Persian word "darvsh," the ultimate source of "dervish," means "religious mendicant." The word is first recorded in English in 1585.

Source: *The American Heritage® Dictionary of the English Language*. Fourth Edition. Copyright © 2000 by Houghton Mifflin Company. Published by the Houghton Mifflin Company. All rights reserved.

**Write a brief character analysis of the old man and his family.**

• The old man and his family are content — even happy.

• The old man and his family ignore the wars and murders and crimes and politics that happen elsewhere.

• The old man and his family have enough. They work hard on their little farm, and they have plenty of food and good things to eat.

• The old man and his family have only 20 acres, but they are enough.

• The old man says that work helps him and his family avoid three evils:

1) boredom
2) vice
3) poverty

• Work, of course, is important because it results in money. Art Linkletter used to interview children on daytime TV. He asked some children what was the secret of happiness. A young boy whose family did not have much money answered, "A steady paycheck."

• Of course, boredom is what Candide and the others complain about at the beginning of this chapter.

• The old man's advice would cure Pococurante's boredom.

- The dervish had some good advice about what not to do. Don't over-think things.
- The good old man has good advice, through the example of himself and his family, about what to do. Work hard, and cultivate your garden.
- The old man's farm is the closest to El Dorado that we have come outside of El Dorado. The good old man here is similar to the good old man of El Dorado.
- Where should we stay? We should stay where we are able to work and to be comfortable and happy. The places where we see that in the novel are El Dorado, the old man's farm, and finally, Candide's farm.
- The old man does not concern himself with politics and philosophy.
- The old man and his family are good hosts.
- The old man and his family are not bored, do not engage in vice, and are not poor.
- Note that the old man and all of his family work. They do not sit back and let one person do all the work. (Cacambo has been doing all the work on the little farm.)

**What happens when Candide and the others begin to work on the small farm?**

- Work can be good. We should note that people in Eldorado worked.
- Good things happen when Candide and the others begin to work on the small farm. From *Candide*:

> "Work then without disputing," said Martin; "it is the only way to render life supportable."

> The little society, one and all, entered into this laudable design and set themselves to exert their different talents. The little piece of ground yielded them a plentiful crop. Cunegund indeed was very ugly, but she became an excellent

hand at pastrywork: Pacquette embroidered; the old woman had the care of the linen. There was none, down to Brother Giroflée, but did some service; he was a very good carpenter, and became an honest man. Pangloss used now and then to say to Candide:

"There is a concatenation of all events in the best of possible worlds; for, in short, had you not been kicked out of a fine castle for the love of Miss Cunegund; had you not been put into the Inquisition; had you not traveled over America on foot; had you not run the Baron through the body; and had you not lost all your sheep, which you brought from the good country of El Dorado, you would not have been here to eat preserved citrons and pistachio nuts."

"Excellently observed," answered Candide; "but let us cultivate our garden."

(Translation by Tobias Smollett)

**Interpret the last words of the short novel: In Lowell Bair's translation: "[...] we must cultivate our garden" (120).**
- Another well-known garden is the Garden of Eden.
- I think it is a positive message. Large amounts of evil exist in the world, but it is possible to be happy in some small part of the world that you cultivate.
- We should note that Candide and the others are not rich.
- Does cultivating your garden mean to turn your back on the world? We should note that Candide and the others are taking action, not turning their back on the world. They are growing food that feeds people. This is our number-one necessity.
- Does cultivating your garden mean to improve a part of the world? I think so, yes. The small farm becomes a place of happiness.

• Candide and the others both work and don't argue.

**What does "meliorism" mean?**

According to <wordnet.princeton.edu/perl/webwn>, "meliorism" is "the belief that the world can be made better by human effort."

**Did Voltaire accept his own advice?**

• Some people may think that cultivating one's garden is not enough. Voltaire himself worked tirelessly as a reformer.

• Cultivating one's garden may mean making at least a part of the world better. Voltaire did that, and because he was a great man, he was able to have a lasting influence on the world.

• We have to say that Voltaire was an intellectual, and it seems that the message of *Candide* may be not to philosophize. Perhaps it is more accurate to say that one ought not to engage in bad philosophy. Voltaire used philosophy to fight injustice.

• Voltaire, like other thinkers of the Enlightenment, believed that human beings can make the world better.

• Voltaire definitely felt that philosophical optimism was a bad philosophy.

• Voltaire definitely realized that evil exists.

• Voltaire apparently felt that we ought to fight against evil.

• The old man and his family and Candide and his group of friends are able to carve out small areas of peace and happiness for themselves.

• Candide and his groups of friends are making the world better. It may appear that they are doing so on a small scale (although growing food is something that absolutely has to be done). Voltaire himself tried to make the world better on a big scale. Voltaire apparently wants each of us to make the world better in our way, to whatever extent we can. We can be happy that Pangloss and Martin do not write books of philosophy. The old man knows nothing of politics in Constantinople because it would not matter if he did. Other people such as Voltaire do pay attention to philosophy and politics, and the world is better off for it.

• We must cultivate our talents. Voltaire had a talent for writing and for satire, and he cultivated his talent. We can be glad he did.

**In _Candide_, Voltaire focuses on how individuals can live their lives in a world of evil. But what about governments? Based on what you have read in the short novel, what features of government would result in less evil in the world?**

• I think that Voltaire would be happy with the Bill of Rights in the Constitution of the United States.

• We have seen slavery in the short novel. Voltaire would prefer that governments abolish slavery.

• We have seen religious intolerance in the short novel. Voltaire would prefer that governments allow people to worship as they please.

• We have seen lack of freedom of speech in the short novel. Voltaire would prefer that speech be free.

• We have seen many executions in the short novel. Voltaire would perhaps prefer that capital punishment be abolished.

• We have seen much corruption of police and judges and other people in the short novel. Voltaire would prefer that corruption be against the law — and that the law be enforced.

• We have seen much sexual exploitation of women in the short novel. Voltaire would prefer that sexual exploitation of women be against the law — and that the law be enforced.

• We have seen that Paquette is forced to be a prostitute to make a (poor) living. Voltaire may prefer that a social safety net be implemented so that no woman is forced by economic necessity to be a prostitute.

**Chapter 1 can be seen as a fall from grace (compare the Garden of Eden myth). In Chapter 30, we have another garden. How is Candide's garden similar to and different from the Garden of Eden?**

• In the Garden of Eden, Adam and Eve did not have to work. Candide and the others work very hard indeed.

• The story of Adam and Eve begins in a garden. The story of Candide and the others both begins and ends in a garden.

**Has Candide changed?**

• Candide is much more mature than he was at the beginning of this short novel. Then he was naïve and mainly a philosophical optimist, influenced greatly by Dr. Pangloss.

• Now Candide makes up his own mind. At the end of *Candide*, he takes a middle position between the excessive optimism of Dr. Pangloss and the excessive pessimism of Martin.

• At the end of *Candide*, Candide apparently believes in meliorism. Human beings can make the world better, in least in small areas. We can sometimes be successful in carving out areas of peace and happiness for us in the world. (Of course, we remember that good people such as James the Anabaptist attempted to do this, but bad things happened to him. He died trying to save the life of someone else — someone who was a bad man.)

**Is this the best of all possible worlds?**

• H*LL, NO! It is not the best of all possible worlds if you are looking for a hedonistic paradise with freedom from evil, both natural and moral.

• However, C. S. Lewis and John Hick have good things to say about God's purpose for creating the world. It is good for making and developing souls. It is good for exercising free will. It is not the Heavenly Paradise that I think we would call the best of all possible worlds. In the Heavenly Paradise, our souls are already perfected, and therefore moral evil and natural evil serve no purpose.

• See Appendix B and Appendix C for more information about the ideas of C.S. Lewis and John Hick.

**How does Voltaire criticize Pangloss' philosophy in this short novel?**

• Voltaire greatly criticizes Pangloss' optimistic philosophy:

1) Pangloss says that this is the best of all possible worlds. However, this belief is contradicted by real-world evidence. Over and over, we see natural evil (the Lisbon earthquake) and moral evil (religious intolerance). Despite all the evil that Dr. Pangloss suffers, he continues to retain his belief in philosophical optimism.

2) Pangloss' philosophy encourages quietism: calm acceptance of the world with no attempt to change things. If this is the best of all possible worlds, nothing we can do can make it better, and so we ought to do nothing. Voltaire clearly acknowledges the existence of evil in the world, and he thinks that we ought to do what we can to relieve that evil. John Steinbeck, author of *The Grapes of Wrath*, agrees:

> In February of 1938, floods struck the San Joaquin Valley. To help people, author John Steinbeck worked with Tom Collins, who managed a camp for people who had migrated to California during the Great Depression to look for work. Together, they found a mother and her children. The mother was near starvation because she had given all the food to her children. Mr. Steinbeck walked two miles to a store to buy food for the mother and her children. Some public health nurses who had visited the area had left because they felt that the problem was too big for their efforts to make much improvement. Mr. Steinbeck disagreed with this view, saying that "the argument that one person's effort can't really do anything doesn't seem to apply when you come on a bunch of starving children and you have a little money." In 1939, a university student asked Mr. Steinbeck what was his philosophy of life. Mr. Steinbeck replied, "I don't like people to be hurt or hungry or unnecessarily sad. It's just as simple as that." (In 1940, Mr. Steinbeck did another good deed after being awarded the Pulitzer Prize in Literature for his masterpiece, *The Grapes of Wrath*. The Pulitzer Prize

included a cash award of $1,000, and he gave all of the money to another writer to help him in his career: Ritch Lovejoy.)

Retold in my own words from information found in this book: Catherine Reef, *John Steinbeck*, pp. 82, 85, 151, 122.

**How does Voltaire criticize Martin's philosophy in this short novel?**

• Martin's philosophy is extreme, as is Pangloss', but Martin's extreme pessimism is more believable than Pangloss' extreme optimism. At least, Martin's philosophy recognizes that evil exists.

• The problem with Martin's extreme pessimism, of course, is that good also exists in this world. We have evidence of good in this work with James the Anabaptist early in the novel and with the old man in Chapter 30. In addition, Candide is good, although for much of the novel he is naïve.

• Voltaire also criticizes Martin when Martin thinks that Cacambo is dishonest and ran off with the wealth that Candide gave him instead of rescuing Cunegonde. Instead, Cacambo was honest but ran into bad luck when he was robbed and sold into slavery by a pirate.

• Martin's extreme pessimism and cynicism can also lead to quietism. If everyone is selfish and everything is sh*t, why try to do anything to improve the world?

**What is the parable of the two jars that Achilles recounts in Book 24 of Homer's *Iliad*? Is this a realistic philosophy?**

In Book 24 of Homer's *Iliad*, Achilles tells King Priam that Zeus has two jars from which he dispenses gifts to human beings. One jar is filled with bad things; the other jar is filled with good things. To some people, Zeus gives only bad gifts; to other people Zeus gives both good and bad gifts. To no one does Zeus give only good gifts.

The meaning of this story is very clear. Everyone will experience bad things in his or her life. Some unfortunate people experience only bad things in their lives, while fortunate people will experience much good but also some bad in their lives.

This may seem pessimistic to some people, but it also is true. All of us are mortal, and to mortal creatures death is not optional. This means that all of us will die, and death is usually seen as a bad thing. When death is seen as a good thing, it is because (usually) life is seen as a bad thing — a person's life is so unfortunate that that person longs to die.

The story is true for both Achilles and Priam. They are great human beings with great gifts, but they have suffered. King Priam's city is at war and will fall and Achilles has killed many of King Priam's sons, most notably Hector. Achilles is of course the greatest Achaean warrior, but his best friend, Patroclus, has died. Both of these men — who are enemies to each other and who are the greatest men of their age — have suffered.

Achilles gives Priam good advice — good advice that Achilles has had to learn to accept. Achilles tells Priam about the human condition. We are born, loved ones die, we suffer and grieve, and then we move on with our lives. This is exactly what others have been telling Achilles. They have wanted him to eat, but Achilles has refused to do that. Now we have Achilles serving a meal to Priam and telling him that he must eat. Achilles will give Priam time to mourn and hold a funeral for Hector, and then they will get on with their lives again. Achilles will go to war again because Achilles is a warrior.

In this famous passage, Achilles talks about what human life is like:

> "So the immortals spun our lives that we, we wretched men
> live on to bear such torments — the gods live free of sorrows.
> There are two great jars that stand on the floor of Zeus's halls
> and hold his gifts, our miseries one, the other blessings.
> When Zeus who loves the lightning mixes gifts for a man,
> now he meets with misfortune, now good times in turn.
> When Zeus dispenses gifts from the jar of sorrows only,

he makes a man an outcast — brutal, ravenous hunger
drives him down the face of the shining earth,
stalking far and wide, cursed by gods and men."
(Fagles 24.615-622)

This is a realistic philosophy. For human beings, grief is in store. No one is able to escape grief and death. The best that human beings can hope for is a mixture of good and bad things. Some human beings don't even get that. They just get the bad things. Who is able to escape grief and death? The gods are able to escape death, but even they sometimes feel grief. Thetis grieves that Achilles will soon die. Zeus grieves because his son Sarpedon died. Achilles says that "the gods live free of sorrows" (Fagles 24.617), but that is not quite true.

A Chinese sage was asked to write a poem that would bless a nobleman's house. The sage wrote, "Grandfather Die, Father Die, Son Die." The nobleman was outraged, but the sage explained that the poem offered good wishes. It is best when the grandfather grows old and dies, then the father grows old and dies, and finally the son grows old and dies. It is a tragedy when the son dies before the father. Remember: For humans, death is not optional.

At Ohio University in Athens, Ohio, four Korean students were killed in a car accident. Ohio U arranged a memorial service for the students, which the students' parents attended. One of the fathers of the students thanked the mourners attending the service, then said, "This is not the way it is supposed to be. When a parent dies, you bury them in the ground, but when a child dies, you bury them in your heart." (Source: Ohio University Emeriti Association, compilers, *Ohio University Recollections for the Bicentennial Anniversary: 1804-2004*, p. 72.)

Achilles has learned to accept the human condition, to realize and to accept that all of us will die, including the people we love most.

**In *Candide*, a number of characters — Cunegonde, Pangloss, and the young Baron — are thought to be dead, but are later discovered to be alive. What is Voltaire's purpose in resurrecting these characters?**

• We can look at the characters as symbols of various evils. If so, then their resurrections may mean that Voltaire believes that these traits never truly die.

*Cunegonde*

Beauty does not last; women are victimized sexually; love doesn't last (Candide is shocked by Cunegonde's ugliness, but because he is a good person, he marries her).

*Pangloss*

Pangloss is a symbol of bad ideas. His extreme optimism is not a realistic philosophy.

*The Baron*

The young Baron is a snob. Snobbery has hardly got out of style in our modern world.

• More optimistically, we can say that the world contains surprises, and sometimes those surprises are good. Candide is happy that his friends are alive, even though his friends are not perfect, and even though the young Baron is such a snob that Candide helps to sell him into slavery again.

**Much of *Candide* is about evil, but goodness exists in it as well. What goodness as opposed to evil do we see in this short novel?**

• The old man in Chapter 30 is good. So is his family.

• James (aka Jacques) the Anabaptist is good.

• Candide is good. He married Cunegonde although she is ugly.

• Many of the other characters are good in some way:

*The Old Woman*

The Old Woman helps Candide after he has been whipped in auto-da-fé.

*Cacambo*
Cacamo is loyal and practical, and he is a good advisor to Candide.

• At the end of the short novel, many of the characters are working hard on the farm.

• El Dorado is an ideal society, but ideals are worth trying to achieve, although we will always fall short of accomplishing them.

**How should you lead your life? If you wish to be happy, what can you do, according to *Candide*? Is this good advice?**

• The characters in *Candide* learn to work and to avoid boredom, vice, and poverty:

> Cunegonde becomes an excellent pastry cook.
> Paquette embroiders.
> The old woman takes care of the linen.
> Brother Giroflée becomes a carpenter.
> Everyone else works in the fields.

• You can decide to do the same thing.

**How can you tell right from wrong?**

When you are deciding what is right and what is wrong, here a few things to consider:

*Consequences*

If something will have bad consequences, we probably ought not to do it. If something will have good consequences, we probably ought to do it. This seems obvious. If hitting yourself on the head with a hammer gives you headaches, I recommend that you stop hitting yourself on the head with a hammer. Ask yourself: What are the consequences of what you are thinking about doing?

*The Golden Rule*

Here are two formulations of the Golden Rule, one stated positively, and the other stated negatively:

- Treat other people the way you want to be treated.
- Do not treat other people the way that you do not want to
be treated.

Ask yourself: Is what you are thinking about doing consistent with the Golden Rule?

*Reversibility*

One way to find out if something is morally right is to ask if you want something done to you. You may be thinking that you would like other people to be forced to do something, but would you want to be forced to do that thing?

Let's suppose that you need money desperately and that the only way you can acquire that money is to borrow it and make a lying promise that you will pay the money back although you know that you will never be able to do so. The principle would be this: "When you need money, it's ok to make a lying promise that you will pay the money back although you know that you will never be able to do so." Is this principle moral?

"Reversibility" means that what you want to do to another person, that person can also do to you. (In other words, you "reverse" the situation.) You may be willing to make a lying promise to obtain other people's money, but are you willing to allow other people to make lying promises to you in order to obtain your money? Of course not.

Here's another example of reversibility from *The Dick Van Dyke Show*. In the episode "Punch Thy Neighbor," Rob Petrie's neighbor Jerry Helper teases Rob mercilessly about a "bad" show that Rob wrote for *The Alan Brady Show*. Rob tells Jerry that the teasing isn't funny, but Jerry keeps on teasing. Finally, Rob opens his door and yells outside, "Jerry Helper is a rotten dentist." Then Jerry realizes that the teasing isn't funny. Jerry is willing to tease other people, but he doesn't want to be teased himself.

*Human Beings are Valuable*

To be moral, we ought to treat human beings as valuable, and we ought not to treat other human beings badly. In fancy language, we ought to treat other human beings and ourselves as ends (valuable in themselves) rather than as means (things to be used, then tossed aside). Make sure that what you are thinking about doing treats other people with respect.

The moral philosopher Immanuel Kant formulated a moral rule that he called the categorical imperative. This is one of the ways that he expressed it: "Act in such a way that you treat humanity, whether in your own person or in the person of another, always at the same time as an end and never simply as a means" (*Foundations of the Metaphysics of Morals*, translated by Lewis White Beck).

If you treat another person as a means, then you are using that person. For example, a guy unfortunately might be very nice to a woman, sleep with her, then never call her. In this example, the guy is treating the woman as a means to an orgasm, not as someone valuable in herself.

If you treat other people as ends, then you are treating them as valuable in themselves. For example, you can treat everybody you meet with common courtesy (which, as you probably know, is no longer common). If you see a parent teaching her young child how to cross the street, you can decide to refrain from jaywalking this one time and thus be a role model for the child. You can also refrain from demonstrating power by ordering around waitresses in a restaurant.

As I hope that you can see, our example of making a lying promise to borrow money fails this formulation of the categorical imperative. If you make a lying promise to borrow money, you are using the person you are borrowing from. You are not treating the person as an end; you are treating the person as a means. You value the money more than you value the person.

*Happiness*

Happiness is good. We have to do some things, such as make a living and pay our bills. We ought to do some things, such as exercise and eat healthily. We want to do some things, maybe even things that other people find silly. As long as the things we want to do don't conflict with the things we have to do and the things we ought to do, go ahead and do them. Ask yourself: Will what you are thinking about doing bring happiness to people, including yourself?

*What Would Happen if Everybody Did It?*

If everybody pirates music, what would happen? Chances are, less new music will be written. If musicians can't make a living from their music, they will have to get money from other sources, including jobs that may not allow them enough time to write and perform good music.

**What can *you* do to reduce the amount of evil in the world?**

- Avoid doing evil.
- Don't over-value money — but be competent with it.
- Do good deeds.
- Volunteer.
- Donate.
- Cultivate your garden.
- Science can be a good thing. For example, scientists can help us to do such things as grow more abundant crops and to build buildings that will withstand earthquakes.

# Appendix A: Bibliography

Altman, Linda Jacobs. *Slavery and Abolition in American History*. Berkeley Heights, NJ: Enslow Publications, Inc., 1999.

Bernard, Catherine. *Sojourner Truth: Abolitionist and Women's Rights Activist*. Berkeley Heights, NJ: Enslow Publications, Inc., 2001.

Deedy, John. *A Book of Catholic Anecdotes*. Allen, TX: Thomas More, 1997.

Dolan, Sean. *Juan Ponce de Leon*. Philadelphia, PA: Chelsea House, 1995.

Holman, C. Hugh, and William Harmon. *A Handbook to Literature*. 6th edition. New York: Macmillan Publishing Company, 1992.

Homer. *The Iliad*. Trans. Robert Fagles. New York: Penguin Books, 1990.

Kant, Immanuel. *Foundations of the Metaphysics of Morals*. Trans. Lewis White Beck. Indianapolis, Indiana: Bobbs-Merrill, 1959.

Kendall, Martha E. *Failure is Impossible! The History of American Women's Rights*. Minneapolis, MN: Lerner Publications Company, 2001.

Maurois, Andre. "An Appreciation." *Candide*. By Voltaire. Trans. Lowell Bair. Toronto, New York: Bantam Books, 1981.

Medearis, Angela Shelf, and Michael R. Medearis. *Dance*. New York: Twenty-First Century Books, 1997.

Ohio University Emeriti Association, compilers. *Ohio University Recollections for the Bicentennial Anniversary: 1804-2004*. Athens, OH: Ohio University, 2004.

Reef, Catherine. *John Steinbeck*. New York: Clarion Books, 1996.

Rogers, Fred. *The World According to Mister Rogers*. New York: Hyperion, 2003.

Voltaire. *Candide*. Trans. John Butt. London, England: Penguin Books, 1988.

Voltaire. *Candide*. Trans. Lowell Bair. Toronto, New York: Bantam Books, 1981.

Voltaire. *Candide*. Trans. Tobias Smollett. Summer 2008. <http://en.wikisource.org/wiki/Candide>.

# Appendix B: C. S. Lewis: The Problem of Evil

One person who has addressed the problem of evil in a very interesting way is C. S. Lewis, author of the popular *Chronicles of Narnia* children's books. One of the things he did was to analyze the concepts "omnipotent" and "impossible." In ordinary, unreflective usage, people think of an omnipotent Being as being able to do anything, such as create a stone so heavy He cannot lift it. But no less a theologian than St. Thomas Aquinas writes, "Nothing which implies contradiction falls under the omnipotence of God."

In looking at the concept "impossible," Lewis distinguished between two kinds of impossibilities: conditional and intrinsic. Something is conditionally impossible if there are conditions that make it impossible. For example, we could say, "It is impossible for you to learn Latin unless you study." In other words, "If you don't study, it is impossible for you to learn Latin." The phrase following "if" gives the condition under which learning Latin is impossible.

On the other hand, some things are intrinsically (or absolutely) impossible. For example, a four-sided triangle is intrinsically impossible because triangles are defined as three-sided figures. Another impossible thing is a square circle. Actually, Lewis would object to my use of the word "things" here. According to Lewis, "It remains true that all *things* are possible with God: the intrinsic impossibilities are not things but nonentities."

This analysis clears up the confusion about whether God can create a stone that is so heavy that He cannot lift it. This statement leads to a logical paradox and so is nonsense. According to Lewis, God's "[o]mnipotence means power to do all that is intrinsically possible, not to do the intrinsically impossible. You may attribute miracles to Him, but not nonsense."

One of the things that is intrinsically impossible to do is to create a being that has free will and at the same time does not have free will. Since this is a logical contradiction, it is intrinsically impossible. Thus, if God gave Humankind free will (and the traditional Judaeo-Christian religions say God did do so), then God must leave us free to choose to do either good or evil. Not to do so would be to take away our free will.

What kind of a world would God create if He wished it to be lived in by creatures having free will? Lewis identifies three characteristics that such a world must have:

> 1) If Humankind has free will, then the world must be one in which Humankind has the "freedom to choose: and choice implies the existence of things to choose between." Therefore, we need an environment in which to make choices.

> 2) To exercise our freedom of choice in an environment, the environment must be stable.

> 3) To have a human society, once again the environment must be stable.

What does it mean to have a stable environment? It means that nature must follow fixed laws. This allows both for free choice and for the existence of evil. For example, imagine an environment in which someone decided to hurt a person badly, so he picked up a baseball bat and swung it at the person's head as hard as he could. In a world with fixed natural laws, the baseball bat would of course bust the other person's head open. If God were to fix the world so that no one could ever hurt another person (and thus take away Humankind's free will), then the baseball bat might turn to Jello before hitting the other person.

In addition, if the environment is stable and follows fixed physical laws, then it won't make exceptions for good people. Good people will suffer from diseases just like bad people. Rain will fall on both good and bad people. A good person who is rock climbing and makes a misstep will fall to the ground just as hard as a bad person would.

God's creation of a stable environment is necessary for us to have free will, but it is also necessary for these reasons:

1) Unless nature follows fixed laws, it would be impossible for science to develop, and

2) We communicate with other human beings and become aware of their existence through our use of a common, neutral environment.

What Lewis has shown us is:

1) God cannot do what is intrinsically impossible, such as create a being that has free will and at the same time does not have free will, and

2) God, to provide a suitable environment for His free creatures, must create an environment that is stable and follows fixed laws.

Because of these two things, both moral evil (which man is responsible for through using his free will to choose to do evil) and natural evil (which comes about from nature following natural laws, resulting in tornados, earthquakes, volcanoes, birth defects, etc.) become possible.

**Note**: The quotations by C. S. Lewis that appear in this essay are from his *The Problem of Pain* (London: Geoffrey Bles, 1940).

# Appendix C: John Hick: The Problem of Evil

A theodicy is an attempt to justify the goodness of God despite the presence of evil in the world. John Hick is an important philosopher/theologian who has developed what we can call the "Vale of Soul-Making" theodicy. In it, Hick suggests that the purpose of the universe is not to be a hedonistic paradise (although Heaven may very well be that), but is instead to help us develop souls so that one day we may become worthy of being citizens of Heaven.

Hick begins by contrasting two different views of Humankind, beginning with the view of Saint Augustine (354-430 C.E.), which is called by Hick "the majority report," meaning that very many people believe it. According to Saint Augustine, human free will accounts for much of the evil that we find in the world. This is something that Hick agrees with; however, he does not agree with Saint Augustine's second assertion, which is that at one time Humankind was in a state of perfection, from which it fell. In other words, Saint Augustine believes that God created Humankind perfect, but that through the use of free will, Humankind sinned and stopped being perfect.

This, of course, is one way to interpret the myth of the Garden of Eden. Adam and Eve were perfect, but they were tempted to sin, gave in to this temptation and did sin, and so became not perfect. However, there are other ways to interpret this myth. My own interpretation is that at one time Humankind did not sin — when our ancestors had not acquired the knowledge of good and evil and so were incapable of sinning. However, eventually Humankind achieved sufficient intelligence to know the difference between right and wrong and so became able to sin. (I don't think that a dog sins because a dog is not capable of knowing the difference between right and wrong.)

Instead of accepting this opinion of Saint Augustine's, Hick much prefers what he calls the "minority report" of St. Irenaeus (born in Anatolia, circa 140-60 C.E.; died circa 200 C.E.), a second-century Christian writer. As Hick writes, "Instead of regarding man as having been created by God in a finished state, as a finitely perfect being fulfilling the divine intention for our human level of existence, and then falling disastrously away from this, the minority report sees man as still in process of creation."

An important part of Hick's theodicy is that he recognizes two levels of existence: *Bios* and *Zoe*. *Bios* is mere biological life, whereas *Zoe* is eternal or spiritual life. St. Irenaeus believes that we were created with biological life, and that we are in the process of acquiring eternal or spiritual life.

This view can be supported with passages from the Bible. We are supposed to become "children of God" (*Hebrews* ii. 10) and "fellow heirs with Christ" (*Romans* viii. 17). In addition, this view is compatible with evolution. We know that life probably originated as one-celled creatures in the ocean; therefore, Humankind was not created perfect and whole. Instead, life has evolved to the point where Humankind has achieved enough intelligence to tell right from wrong and has achieved the free will to choose to join the race of decent men or the race of indecent men (using Viktor Frankl's terminology in *Man's Search for Meaning*).

Hick does make a value judgment in his theodicy. He writes, "The value-judgment that is implicitly being invoked here is that one who has attained to goodness by meeting and eventually mastering temptations, and thus by rightly making responsible choices in concrete situations, is good in a richer and more valuable sense than would be one created *ab initio* in a state of either innocence or virtue."

God could have created us morally perfect, if He had wished. However, He would have had to create us without free will — we would be like robots that are programmed always to do good and never to do evil. It is much more morally valuable to have a human being who freely chooses to do the right thing than to have a robot that is forced always to do the right thing.

Hick also points out, "Man is in process of becoming the perfected being whom God is seeking to create. However, this is not taking place — it is important to add — by a natural and inevitable evolution, but through a hazardous adventure in individual freedom."

Many people might think that the world ought to be becoming better and better as Humankind becomes more and more perfect. However, that is not the case. The move toward becoming a perfected being is happening in individuals, not in Humankind as a whole.

In fact, Hick specifically states, "Because this is a pilgrimage within the life of each individual, rather than a racial evolution, the progressive fulfilment of God's purpose does not entail any corresponding progressive improvement in the moral state of the world."

In addition, Hick points out a common mistake (made by David Hume, among others): "They think of God's relation to the earth on the model of a human being building a cage for a pet animal to dwell in." When these critics of theism look at the world, they note its imperfections and criticize it because of them. They believe that if God really were omnipotent and omnibenevolent, then He would have made the Earth a hedonistic paradise.

Hick writes, "Men are not to be thought of on the analogy of animal pets, whose life is to be made as agreeable as possible, but rather on the analogy of human children, who are to grow to adulthood in an environment whose primary and overriding purpose is not immediate pleasure but the realizing of the most valuable potentialities of human personality."

As you can see, Hick believes that the world was made not to be a source of endless delights for Humankind, but was made in order for us to develop souls. What kind of world is necessary in order to make souls? Suppose I were to ask you: What is more important?

Pleasure, or Moral Integrity?
Pleasure, or Unselfishness?
Pleasure, or Compassion?
Pleasure, or Courage?
Pleasure, or Humor?
Pleasure, or Reverence for the Truth?
Pleasure, or the Capacity to Love?

I would hope that you would agree that pleasure is less important than the other qualities listed above. To help us develop those better qualities, God has not created a hedonistic paradise on this Earth, but instead He has created a world in which there is evil, yes, but a world in which we can — if we choose — develop the better qualities listed above.

Hick's theodicy includes these themes: free will, and harmony. We see the harmony in a World (Heaven) to come in which Humankind (who have become citizens of Heaven) has achieved the better qualities listed above. According to Hick, "The good that outshines all ill is not a paradise long since lost but a kingdom which is yet to come in its full glory and permanence."

By the way, the phrase "the vale of Soul-making" comes from a letter written by English poet John Keats to his siblings in April 1819.

**Note**: The quotations by John Hick that appear in this essay are from his *Evil and the God of Love*, revised edition by John Hick (copyright 1966 and 1978).

# Appendix D: Peter Singer: The Argument to Assist

**• What are "absolute poverty" and "absolute affluence"?**

Absolute poverty is when you can't provide yourself and your dependents with the necessities of life: food, shelter, and clothing. Many people in third-world nations suffer from absolute poverty.

Absolute affluence is when you have a significant amount of income above what is needed to provide yourself and your dependents with the necessities of life. Many people in Europe, North America, and Asia have absolute affluence.

Part of Singer's point is that people in first-world nations don't do enough to help people in third-world nations. This comes out in his discussion of the percentage of GNP that first-world nations spend on developmental assistance to third-world nations.

**• What causes absolute poverty?**

Singer believes that the World produces enough food to feed its population. (The Vatican agrees with this.) One problem is that we feed grain to cattle and other animals. This is an inefficient use of protein and food, as it takes a lot of pounds of grain to produce one pound of animal protein. If we were to become vegetarians, this would make a lot of grain available for purposes other than feeding cattle.

In general, Singer believes that the problem is one of distribution, not of production. The world produces enough food, but it isn't distributed to those who need it.

In addition, there may be economic exploitation of third-world countries by first-world countries.

**• Is it a consequence of my spending money on a luxury item that someone in the third world dies?**

According to Singer and consequentialism, yes. If you don't buy the luxury item and instead use the money to feed a starving person and save his life, then you have done a good thing. But if you do buy a luxury item and don't use the money to save the life of a person in a third-world nation, then you have done a bad thing. What you do with your money is up to you, but you are responsible for the consequences of your actions.

**• What is the "non-consequentialist view of responsibility"? (A theory of rights with an appended distinction between acts and omissions — killing and letting die.)**

According to a non-consequentialist view of responsibility, I can spend my money on a luxury item as long as my action does not leave the person in the third-world nation worse off than he was before. In other words, there is a distinction between killing and letting die. If I murder a person in a third-world nation by shooting him with a gun, then I am responsible for that person's death, but if that person dies because I didn't give money to charity, then I am not responsible for that person's death.

**• Why does Singer think we ought to reject the "non-consequentialist view of responsibility"?**

Singer thinks that it is an individual theory, based on people living separately in a state of nature. However, Singer knows that we are social creatures and that many of our accomplishments have come about because we are social creatures.

**• Explain how Singer arrives at the conclusion that "We ought to prevent some absolute poverty." What "plausible principle" does he use to get his argument started?**

Singer uses an analogy. On his walk to work is an ornamental pond. Suppose he were to see a child drowning in the pool. Shouldn't he rescue the child even if it is inconvenient to him? For example, even if he has to get his pants dirty and be late for a lecture, wouldn't we think that he ought to rescue the child? Of course we do. Singer believes that this situation is analogous to helping a person in a third-world nation.

The plausible principle he arrives at is this: "If something is in our power to prevent something bad from happening, without thereby sacrificing anything of comparable moral significance, we ought to do it."

• **Singer says that this plausible principle will please consequentialists, but non-consequentialists should accept it, too. Who does he have in mind here and why should they accept it? Why is the "plausible principle" not open to many of the standard counterexamples to consequentialism?**

Non-consequentialists will be pleased with the theory because of the part in the middle: "If something is in our power to prevent something bad from happening, <u>without thereby sacrificing anything of comparable moral significance</u>, we ought to do it." As Kantians know, things other than consequences are important; for example, keeping promises, not lying, etc. This plausible principle does not require us to lie or break a promise if doing so will have a good consequence.

• **What would happen if we took Singer's argument seriously and began to live our lives by it?**

It would have a big impact on our lives. We would give much, much more money to charity. Instead of having a second car or a second home, we would give the money to charity (if you think that saving someone's life is more important than having a second car or a second home).

• **Can we escape our obligation to help by saying that we ought to take care of our own first?**

We will not let our own family fall into absolute poverty while we help others. To do so would mean sacrificing something of comparable moral significance. However, we need to recognize that other people need help and that absolute poverty mainly exists in the poor nations.

• **Can we escape our obligation to help by appealing to property rights?**

Singer thinks that the theory of property rights leaves too much to chance. For example, you may be rich or poor because of chance. If you are born into a wealthy family, you will be rich. If you are born into a poor family, you will be poor. If you didn't know which family you would be born into ahead of time, wouldn't you hope that the rich would share with the poor?

• **What is triage, and what is the argument that tries to show that we ought to adopt it as a policy toward the poor countries?**

Triage is a way of dealing with the wounded in wartime when medical resources are limited. The wounded are divided into three groups: 1) those who will probably get better without medical assistance, 2) those who will probably get better with medical assistance, and 3) those who will probably not get better with medical assistance, Because medical resources are limited, the idea is to make the best use of them by focusing on people in the middle group. That way, the greatest number of people will live.

People who make use of this argument believe that the world is like a lifeboat. If too many get on the lifeboat, it will sink and everyone will die. Therefore, we should focus on helping only those we think it possible to save without thereby jeopardizing ourselves. In this way of reasoning, people think that if we help the poorest of the poor, we will only be setting up conditions for even more people to die in the future. People will live to have lots of children, and the children will die.

• **What is a "demographic transition"? What role does it play in Singer's argument against triage?**

As countries become affluent, there is a demographic transition. Instead of having lots of children because so many die in infancy, people begin to have fewer children. Because of this, we need not be setting up conditions for even greater misery in the future. Singer does say, however, that we need to consider population growth in the kind of aid we give, and that we ought to give the kinds of aid that lead to the desired demographic transition.

- **What kinds of aid ought we to give?**

We ought to give the kinds of aid that will result in the desired demographic transition. Instead of simply giving away food, we might instead educate farmers about how to grow more plentiful crops or we might give away food-producing animals.

**Note**: The quotations by Peter Singer that appear in this essay are from his *Practical Ethics* (Cambridge, New York: Cambridge University Press, 1980).

# Appendix E: Sample Short Reaction Memos

The questions in this short guide can be used in discussions; however, they can also be used for short reaction memos. For example, I do this at Ohio University. See below for the assignment and sample short reaction memos.

*How Do I Complete the Reaction Memo Assignments?*

During the quarter, you will have to write a series of short memos in which you write about the readings you have been assigned.

Each memo should be at least 250 words, not counting long quotations from the work of literature. Include a word count for each memo, although that is not normally part of the memo format.

Following the memo heading (To, From, Re, Date, Words), write the question you are answering and the part of the book that the question applies to.

You may answer one question or more than one question. I will supply you with a list of questions that you may answer

Note that a Works Cited list is needed if you use quotations.

For examples from my Great Books courses at Ohio University in Athens, Ohio, see the following:

**To: David Bruce**
**From: Jane Student**
**Re: *Odyssey*, Book 12 Reaction Memo**
**Date: Put Today's Date Here**
**Words: 323**
***Odyssey*, Book 12: Is Odysseus a bad leader?**

This is an important question in the *Odyssey*. After all, Odysseus leads 12 ships and many men to Troy, but the ships are all destroyed and all of his men die and he returns home to Ithaca alone. Who is responsible for the deaths of Odysseus' men? Is Odysseus responsible for their deaths, or do the men bear some responsibility for their own deaths? Many readers prefer Odysseus, the great individualist, to Aeneas, the man who founds the Roman people, but then they realize that all of Odysseus' men died, while Aeneas succeeded in bringing many Trojans to Italy. When readers think of that, they begin to have a greater respect for Aeneas.

From the beginning of the *Odyssey*, this has been an issue. The bard says that the men perished because of the "recklessness of their own ways" (1.8). However, we notice that Odysseus is asleep at odd times. In Book 10, Aeolus gives Odysseus a bag in which the contrary winds have been tied up. This allows Odysseus to sail to Ithaca safely. However, they reach the island and see smoke rising from the fires, Odysseus goes to sleep and his men open the bag, letting the contrary winds escape, and the ship is blown back to King Aeolus' island. Similarly, in Book 12, on the island of the Sun-god, Odysseus is asleep when his men sacrifice the Sun-god's cattle.

It does seem that Odysseus does not bear the blame for his men's death. In many cases, they do perish through their own stupidity. In other cases, of course, they die during war or during adventures, but in those times, Odysseus was with them, and he could have died, too.

One other thing to think about is that Odysseus is telling his own story. Could he be lying? After all, some of the adventures he relates are pretty incredible. (Probably not. The gods vouch for some of what he says.)

Works Cited

Homer. *The Odyssey*. Trans. Robert Fagles. New York: Penguin Books, 1996. Print.

To: David Bruce

From: Jane Student

Re: *Inferno*, Canto 1 Reaction Memo

Date: Put Today's Date Here

Words: 263

*Inferno*, Canto 1

• **What do you need to be a member of the Afterlife in Dante's** *Inferno*?

To be a member of the afterlife in Hell, you must meet a number of criteria:

1) You must be dead.

2) You must be an unrepentant sinner.

3) You must be a dead, unrepentant sinner by 1300.

Of course, only dead people — with a few exceptions such as Dante the Pilgrim — can be found in the Inferno.

Only unrepentant sinners can be found in the Inferno. Everyone has sinned, but sinners who repented their sins are found in Purgatory or Paradise, not in the Inferno.

Dante set his *Divine Comedy* in 1300, so the characters who appear in it are dead in 1300.

*Inferno*, Canto 1

• **What does it mean to repent?**

A sinner who repents regrets having committed the sin. The repentant sinner vows not to commit the sin again, and he or she does his or her best not to commit the sin again.

*Inferno*, Canto 1

• **What is the geography of Hell? In** *The Divine Comedy*, **where is Hell located?**

Hell is located straight down. We will find out later that when Lucifer was thrown out of Paradise, he fell to the Earth, ending up at the center of the Earth. The center of the Earth is the lowest part of Hell. Lucifer created the Mountain of Purgatory when he hit the Earth.

To: David Bruce
From: Jane Student
Re: *Candide*, Ch. 26-30
Date: Today's Date
Words: 368

**Ch. 30: Write a brief character analysis of the old man and his family.**

When Candide and his friends meet the old man, the old man is "sitting in front of his door beneath an arbor of orange trees, enjoying the fresh air" (119). The old man basically ignores politics that he cannot influence. Some people have recently been killed in Constantinople, and the old man does not even know their names. However, the old man does enjoy some material things, including good food, and he enjoys hospitality.

The old man invites Candide and his friends to enjoy some refreshments inside his house. They are served with "several kinds of fruit-favored drinks" and "boiled cream with pieces of candied citron in it, oranges, lemons, limes, pineapples, pistachio nuts, and mocha coffee" (119). The old man and his family have an abundance of food, but although Candide wonders if the old man has an enormous farm, the old man tells him, "I have only twenty acres of land, which my children and I cultivate. Our work keeps us free of three great evils: boredom, vice, and poverty" (119).

From this brief encounter, we learn several things:

- The old man and his family are content — even happy.

- The old man and his family ignore the wars and murders and crimes that happen elsewhere.

- The old man and his family have enough. They work hard on their little farm, and they have plenty of food and good things to eat.

• The old man and his family have only 20 acres, but 20 acres
are enough.

Candide and his friends decide to emulate the old man and his
family. Each of them begins to work hard on their little farm.
Cunegonde learns to make pastry, Paquette begins to embroider, and
the old woman does the laundry and repairs the linen. Brother Giroflée
becomes a carpenter, and Candide and the others grow "abundant
crops" (120). At the end of the short novel, the group of friends seem to
have come the closest they can to happiness in a world filled with evil,
but it does take an effort on their part. As Candide says in the short
novel's last words, "... we must cultivate our garden" (120).

Works Cited

Voltaire. *Candide*. Trans. Lowell Bair. New York: Bantam Books,
1981. Print.

To: David Bruce

From: Jane Student

Re: *A Connecticut Yankee in King Arthur's Court*, Ch. 1-4 Reaction Memo

Date: Put Today's Date Here

Words: 286

## CH. 3: "KNIGHTS OF THE TABLE ROUND"

• **What hints do we have of the relationship between Queen Guenever and Sir Launcelot?**

Some hanky-panky is going on between Sir Launcelot and King Arthur's wife, Queen Guenever. Some six or eight prisoners address her, and they tell her that they have been captured by Sir Kay the Seneschal. Immediately, surprise and astonishment are felt by everybody present. The queen looks disappointed because she had hoped that the prisoners were captured by Sir Launcelot.

As it turns out, they were. Sir Launcelot first rescued Sir Kay from some attackers, then he took Sir Kay's armor and horse and captured more knights. All of these prisoners were actually captured by Sir Launcelot, not by Sir Kay at all.

Two passages let us know that something is going on between Sir Launcelot and Queen Guenever:

1. The first is subtle; she looks disappointed when Sir Kay says that he captured the knights: "Surprise and astonishment flashed from face to face all over the house; the queen's gratified smile faded out at the name of Sir Kay, and she looked disappointed ..." (503).

2. The other is much more overt and occurs after Guenever learns that the knight who really captured the prisoners was Sir Launcelot: "Well, it was touching to see the queen blush and smile, and look embarrassed and happy, and fling furtive glances at Sir Launcelot that would have got him shot in Arkansas, to a dead certainty" (503).

Works Cited

Twain, Mark. *Four Complete Novels*. New York: Gramercy Books, 1982. Print.


159

# Appendix F: Paper Topics

• Explain the ending of *Candide*. What does it mean when Candide says that "we must cultivate our garden" (120)?

• Much of *Candide* is about evil, but goodness exists in the short novel. Examine the theme of goodness in *Candide*.

• Write a character analysis of a major character from *Candide*.

• Compare and contrast two important characters from *Candide*.

• Analyze Candide's advisors.

• In *Candide*, what is Voltaire's attitude toward religion?

• In *Candide*, how does Voltaire answer the question, "What is the meaning of life?" Or does he answer that question? Or: In *Candide*, how does Voltaire answer the question, "How ought one to live in a world that is filled with evil?" Or does he answer that question?

• In *Candide*, how does Voltaire criticize the belief that this is the best of all possible worlds? Based on your reading of the novel, what can we do to make the world better?

• Write a feminist critique of *Candide*. How does it present women and the concerns of women? (Note: "woman" is singular, and "women" is plural.)

• Discuss the female characters in *Candide*.

• Compare and contrast Eldorado, Paris, and Candide's farm at the end of the short novel.

• Much moral evil exists in *Candide*. Explain how the American Bill of Rights, if fairly enforced, would prevent much of that moral evil.

Note: Put the titles of short novels and novels in italics. E.g., *Candide*, *Pride and Prejudice*, and *A Connecticut Yankee in King Arthur's Court*.

# Appendix G: Paper Hints

- **Explain the ending of *Candide*. What does it mean when Candide says that "we must cultivate our garden" (120)?**
  - Cultivating the garden shows that good places on earth are possible.
  - By cultivating the garden, Candide and his friends are helping to feed the world.
  - Working in the garden helps to banish three evils: boredom, vice, and poverty.
  - Ch. 30 can be compared with ch. 1. In ch. 1, it is as if Candide is thrown out of the Garden of Eden. He loses his innocence in the short novel, which is like eating from the Tree of Knowledge of Good and Evil. Candide learns about both good and evil. (Eating from the Tree of Knowledge of Good and Evil may be a good thing. Think of a dog stealing food. The dog does not feel guilty because it does not understand good and evil. A human being who steals food should feel guilty.)
  - Perhaps the reader can compare and contrast three places: Eldorado, Paris, and the garden in ch. 30. The garden would be in the middle, with Eldorado almost completely good and Paris almost completely evil. (Citizens in Eldorado are not allowed to leave.)
- **Much of *Candide* is about evil, but goodness exists in the short novel. Examine the theme of goodness in *Candide*.**
  - James (aka Jacques) the Anabaptist is a character who is very good.
  - During the earthquake and the storm at sea, most people who can are trying to help people who need help.
  - The old man in Eldorado and the old man in ch. 30 are good.
  - Eldorado is good.
  - The dervish is actually helpful, despite being rude.

- Cultivating the garden shows that good places on earth are possible.

- By cultivating the garden, Candide and his friends are helping to feed the world.

- Voltaire in his personal life was a reformer. (With the right government, goodness on earth can be much more widespread.)

- The old woman and Cacambo are both very helpful, although they are not perfect.

- Martin is wrong about Cacambo, who did not run away with the money but who did try to rescue Cunegonde.

- **Write a character analysis of a major character from *Candide*.**

- Many characters are important: Candide, the old woman, Dr. Pangloss, Cunegonde, Martin, Cacambo.

- Candide changes. He starts out optimistic, then he becomes a realist. (I don't see him as a pessimist, although he certainly recognizes the existence of evil.) For example: In ch. 19 Candide tells Dr. Pangloss that he will have to renounce optimism in the end.

- Cunegonde could be an interesting character to write about, especially when one examines her flaws. She lies about having sex with Don Issachar and the Grand Inquisitor. She faints on the couch, not on the floor. She wonders how she will find more jewels after hers are stolen.

- **Compare and contrast two or more important characters from *Candide*.**

- Here students can write about foils. Dr. Pangloss and Martin are foils.

- Here students can write about the old woman and Cacambo, both of whom are advisors to Candide.

- The stories of Cunegonde and the old woman parallel each other.

- **Analyze Candide's advisors.**

- Candide's advisers include Dr. Pangloss, Martin, the old woman, Cacambo, the dervish, and the old man of ch. 30.

• **In *Candide*, what is Voltaire's attitude toward religion?**

• Voltaire is a Deist.

• The religion of Eldorado is Deism.

• Voltaire is very skeptical of organized religion, and he sees much corruption among people who consider themselves religious.

• The Grand Inquisitor, Don Issachar, auto-da-fés.

• The Franciscan friar who stole Cunegonde's jewels.

• The Jews don't pay Candide what his jewels and animals (horses) are worth.

• The Jesuits in South America are taking advantage of the native people.

• **In *Candide*, how does Voltaire answer the question, "What is the meaning of life?" Or does he answer that question? Or: In *Candide*, how does Voltaire answer the question, "How ought one to live in a world that is filled with evil?" Or does he answer that question?**

• Perhaps here the better question would be, "How ought one to live in a world that is filled with evil?"

• Voltaire seems to believe in actions, not words. (However, words — as in satire — can bring about actions.)

• One ought to be aware of evil, but one ought to do good.

• By being aware of evil, one can better protect oneself against it. (Candide would not spend his money so freely.)

• One ought to cultivate one's garden.

• One ought to cultivate one's talents.

• **In *Candide*, how does Voltaire criticize the belief that this is the best of all possible worlds?**

• Natural evil, and Moral evil.

• Misuse of religion, power, sex, and money. — Major THEMES to write about.

• Many, many episodes.

• Candide is kicked out — literally — of Westphalia.

- Candide leaves Eldorado voluntarily.
- The great Lisbon earthquake.
- Religious hypocrisy and auto-da-fés.
- **Write a feminist critique of *Candide*. How does it present women and the concerns of women?**
- The old woman.
- Cunegonde.
- Paquette.
- Sex is used to survive.
- Lots of rape.
- The pirates.
- Women are treated badly.
- Women in Eldorado. Women in the garden in ch. 30.
- Sailor and the prostitute.
- Slavery, including sexual slavery.
- Women can also be fools. Character flaws of Cunegonde and the old woman and Paquette.
- Students can also write about the strengths of the women characters in *Candide*.
- **Discuss the female characters in *Candide*.**
- The women are sexual objects when young, and laborers when old.
- The women lie a lot.
- The women sometimes or often don't accept responsibility for themselves. Often, they see themselves as victims only. (Of course, often they are victims.)
- Students can write that women are treated badly at all times and all places. (But is this true?) Students can write about the strengths of the women characters in *Candide*. Students can do both things in one paper.
- Cunegonde sends the old woman to rescue Candide.

# Appendix H: About the Author

It was a dark and stormy night. Suddenly a cry rang out, and on a hot summer night in 1954, Josephine, wife of Carl Bruce, gave birth to a boy — me. Unfortunately, this young married couple allowed Reuben Saturday, Josephine's brother, to name their first-born. Reuben, aka "The Joker," decided that Bruce was a nice name, so he decided to name me Bruce Bruce. I have gone by my middle name — David — ever since.

Being named Bruce David Bruce hasn't been all bad. Bank tellers remember me very quickly, so I don't often have to show an ID. It can be fun in charades, also. When I was a counselor as a teenager at Camp Echoing Hills in Warsaw, Ohio, a fellow counselor gave the signs for "sounds like" and "two words," then she pointed to a bruise on her leg twice. Bruise Bruise? Oh yeah, Bruce Bruce is the answer!

Uncle Reuben, by the way, gave me a haircut when I was in kindergarten. He cut my hair short and shaved a small bald spot on the back of my head. My mother wouldn't let me go to school until the bald spot grew out again.

Of all my brothers and sisters (six in all), I am the only transplant to Athens, Ohio. I was born in Newark, Ohio, and have lived all around Southeastern Ohio. However, I moved to Athens to go to Ohio University and have never left.

At Ohio U, I never could make up my mind whether to major in English or Philosophy, so I got a bachelor's degree with a double major in both areas, then I added a Master of Arts degree in English and a Master of Arts degree in Philosophy. Yes, I have my MAMA degree.

Currently, and for a long time to come (I eat fruits and veggies), I am spending my retirement writing books such as *Nadia Comaneci: Perfect 10*, *The Funniest People in Dance*, *Homer's* Iliad: *A Retelling in Prose*, and *William Shakespeare's* Othello: *A Retelling in Prose*.

By the way, my sister Brenda Kennedy writes romances such as *A New Beginning* and *Shattered Dreams*.

# Appendix I: Some Other Books by David Bruce

**Discussion Guide Series**

*Dante's* Inferno: *A Discussion Guide*

*Dante's* Paradise: *A Discussion Guide*

*Dante's* Purgatory: *A Discussion Guide*

*Forrest Carter's* The Education of Little Tree: *A Discussion Guide*

*Homer's* Iliad: *A Discussion Guide*

*Homer's* Odyssey: *A Discussion Guide*

*Jane Austen's* Pride and Prejudice: *A Discussion Guide*

*Jerry Spinelli's* Maniac Magee: *A Discussion Guide*

*Jerry Spinelli's* Stargirl: *A Discussion Guide*

*Jonathan Swift's "A Modest Proposal": A Discussion Guide*

*Lloyd Alexander's* The Black Cauldron: *A Discussion Guide*

*Lloyd Alexander's* The Book of Three: *A Discussion Guide*

*Mark Twain's* Adventures of Huckleberry Finn: *A Discussion Guide*

*Mark Twain's* The Adventures of Tom Sawyer: *A Discussion Guide*

*Mark Twain's* A Connecticut Yankee in King Arthur's Court: *A Discussion Guide*

*Mark Twain's* The Prince and the Pauper: *A Discussion Guide*

*Nancy Garden's* Annie on My Mind: *A Discussion Guide*

*Nicholas Sparks'* A Walk to Remember: *A Discussion Guide*

*Virgil's* Aeneid: *A Discussion Guide*

*Virgil's "The Fall of Troy": A Discussion Guide*

*Voltaire's* Candide: *A Discussion Guide*

*William Shakespeare's* 1 Henry IV: *A Discussion Guide*

*William Shakespeare's* Macbeth: *A Discussion Guide*

*William Shakespeare's* A Midsummer Night's Dream: *A Discussion Guide*

*William Shakespeare's* Romeo and Juliet: *A Discussion Guide*

*William Sleator's* Oddballs*: A Discussion Guide*

**Retellings of a Classic Work of Literature**

Arden of Faversham*: A Retelling*

*Ben Jonson's* The Alchemist: *A Retelling*

*Ben Jonson's* The Arraignment, or Poetaster: *A Retelling*

*Ben Jonson's* Bartholomew Fair: *A Retelling*

*Ben Jonson's* The Case is Altered: *A Retelling*

*Ben Jonson's* Catiline's Conspiracy: *A Retelling*

*Ben Jonson's* The Devil is an Ass: *A Retelling*

*Ben Jonson's* Epicene: *A Retelling*

*Ben Jonson's* Every Man in His Humor: *A Retelling*

*Ben Jonson's* Every Man Out of His Humor: *A Retelling*

*Ben Jonson's* The Fountain of Self-Love, or Cynthia's Revels: *A Retelling*

*Ben Jonson's* The Magnetic Lady, or Humors Reconciled: *A Retelling*

*Ben Jonson's* The New Inn, or The Light Heart: *A Retelling*

*Ben Jonson's* Sejanus' Fall: *A Retelling*

*Ben Jonson's* The Staple of News: *A Retelling*

*Ben Jonson's* A Tale of a Tub: *A Retelling*

*Ben Jonson's* Volpone, or the Fox: *A Retelling*

*Christopher Marlowe's Complete Plays: Retellings*

*Christopher Marlowe's* Dido, Queen of Carthage: *A Retelling*

*Christopher Marlowe's* Doctor Faustus: *Retellings of the 1604 A-Text and of the 1616 B-Text*

*Christopher Marlowe's* Edward II: *A Retelling*

*Christopher Marlowe's* The Massacre at Paris: *A Retelling*

*Christopher Marlowe's* The Rich Jew of Malta: *A Retelling*

*Christopher Marlowe's* Tamburlaine, Parts 1 and 2: *Retellings*

*Dante's* Divine Comedy: *A Retelling in Prose*

*Dante's* Inferno: *A Retelling in Prose*

*Dante's* Purgatory: *A Retelling in Prose*

*Dante's* Paradise: *A Retelling in Prose*

The Famous Victories of Henry V: *A Retelling*

*From the* Iliad *to the* Odyssey*: A Retelling in Prose of Quintus of* Smyrna's Posthomerica

*George Chapman, Ben Jonson, and John Marston's* Eastward Ho! *A Retelling*

*George Peele's* The Arraignment of Paris: *A Retelling*

*George Peele's* The Battle of Alcazar: *A Retelling*

*George Peele's* David and Bathsheba, and the Tragedy of Absalom: *A Retelling*

*George Peele's* Edward I: *A Retelling*

*George Peele's* The Old Wives' Tale: *A Retelling*

George-a-Greene: *A Retelling*

The History of King Leir: *A Retelling*

*Homer's* Iliad: *A Retelling in Prose*

*Homer's* Odyssey: *A Retelling in Prose*

*J.W. Gent.'s* The Valiant Scot: *A Retelling*

*Jason and the Argonauts: A Retelling in Prose of Apollonius of* Rhodes' Argonautica

*John Ford: Eight Plays Translated into Modern English*

*John Ford's* The Broken Heart: *A Retelling*

*John Ford's* The Fancies, Chaste and Noble: *A Retelling*

*John Ford's* The Lady's Trial: *A Retelling*

*John Ford's* The Lover's Melancholy: *A Retelling*

*John Ford's* Love's Sacrifice: *A Retelling*

*John Ford's* Perkin Warbeck: *A Retelling*

*John Ford's* The Queen: *A Retelling*

*John Ford's* 'Tis Pity She's a Whore: *A Retelling*

*John Lyly's* Campaspe: *A Retelling*

*John Lyly's* Endymion, The Man in the Moon: *A Retelling*

*John Lyly's* Galatea: *A Retelling*

*John Lyly's* Love's Metamorphosis: *A Retelling*

*John Lyly's* Midas: *A Retelling*

*John Lyly's* Mother Bombie: *A Retelling*

*John Lyly's* Sappho and Phao: *A Retelling*

*John Lyly's* The Woman in the Moon: *A Retelling*

*John Webster's* The White Devil: *A Retelling*

King Edward III: *A Retelling*

Mankind: *A Medieval Morality Play* (A Retelling)

*Margaret Cavendish's* The Unnatural Tragedy: *A Retelling*

The Merry Devil of Edmonton: *A Retelling*

The Summoning of Everyman: *A Medieval Morality Play* (A Retelling)

*Robert Greene's* Friar Bacon and Friar Bungay: *A Retelling*

The Taming of a Shrew: *A Retelling*

*Tarlton's Jests: A Retelling*

*Thomas Middleton's* A Chaste Maid in Cheapside: *A Retelling*

*Thomas Middleton's* Women Beware Women: *A Retelling*

*Thomas Middleton and Thomas Dekker's* The Roaring Girl: *A Retelling*

*Thomas Middleton and William Rowley's* The Changeling: *A Retelling*

*The Trojan War and Its Aftermath: Four Ancient Epic Poems*

*Virgil's* Aeneid: *A Retelling in Prose*

*William Shakespeare's 5 Late Romances: Retellings in Prose*

*William Shakespeare's 10 Histories: Retellings in Prose*

*William Shakespeare's 11 Tragedies: Retellings in Prose*

*William Shakespeare's 12 Comedies: Retellings in Prose*

*William Shakespeare's 38 Plays: Retellings in Prose*

*William Shakespeare's* 1 Henry IV, aka Henry IV, Part 1: *A Retelling in Prose*

*William Shakespeare's* 2 Henry IV, aka Henry IV, Part 2: *A Retelling in Prose*

*William Shakespeare's* 1 Henry VI, aka Henry VI, Part 1: *A Retelling in Prose*

*William Shakespeare's* 2 Henry VI, aka Henry VI, Part 2: *A Retelling in Prose*

*William Shakespeare's* 3 Henry VI, aka Henry VI, Part 3: *A Retelling in Prose*

*William Shakespeare's* All's Well that Ends Well: *A Retelling in Prose*

*William Shakespeare's* Antony and Cleopatra: *A Retelling in Prose*

*William Shakespeare's* As You Like It: *A Retelling in Prose*

*William Shakespeare's* The Comedy of Errors: *A Retelling in Prose*

*William Shakespeare's* Coriolanus: *A Retelling in Prose*

*William Shakespeare's* Cymbeline: *A Retelling in Prose*

*William Shakespeare's* Hamlet: *A Retelling in Prose*

*William Shakespeare's* Henry V: *A Retelling in Prose*

*William Shakespeare's* Henry VIII: *A Retelling in Prose*

*William Shakespeare's* Julius Caesar: *A Retelling in Prose*

*William Shakespeare's* King John: *A Retelling in Prose*

*William Shakespeare's* King Lear: *A Retelling in Prose*

*William Shakespeare's* Love's Labor's Lost: *A Retelling in Prose*

*William Shakespeare's* Macbeth: *A Retelling in Prose*

*William Shakespeare's* Measure for Measure: *A Retelling in Prose*

*William Shakespeare's* The Merchant of Venice: *A Retelling in Prose*

*William Shakespeare's* The Merry Wives of Windsor: *A Retelling in Prose*

*William Shakespeare's* A Midsummer Night's Dream: *A Retelling in Prose*

*William Shakespeare's* Much Ado About Nothing: *A Retelling in Prose*

*William Shakespeare's* Othello: *A Retelling in Prose*

*William Shakespeare's* Pericles, Prince of Tyre: *A Retelling in Prose*

*William Shakespeare's* Richard II: *A Retelling in Prose*

*The Funniest People in Art: 250 Anecdotes*

*The Funniest People in Books: 250 Anecdotes*

*The Funniest People in Books, Volume 2: 250 Anecdotes*

*The Funniest People in Books, Volume 3: 250 Anecdotes*

*The Funniest People in Comedy: 250 Anecdotes*

*The Funniest People in Dance: 250 Anecdotes*

*The Funniest People in Families: 250 Anecdotes*

*The Funniest People in Families, Volume 2: 250 Anecdotes*

*The Funniest People in Families, Volume 3: 250 Anecdotes*

*The Funniest People in Families, Volume 4: 250 Anecdotes*

*The Funniest People in Families, Volume 5: 250 Anecdotes*

*The Funniest People in Families, Volume 6: 250 Anecdotes*

*The Funniest People in Movies: 250 Anecdotes*

*The Funniest People in Music: 250 Anecdotes*

*The Funniest People in Music, Volume 2: 250 Anecdotes*

*The Funniest People in Music, Volume 3: 250 Anecdotes*

*The Funniest People in Neighborhoods: 250 Anecdotes*

*The Funniest People in Relationships: 250 Anecdotes*

*The Funniest People in Sports: 250 Anecdotes*

*The Funniest People in Sports, Volume 2: 250 Anecdotes*

*The Funniest People in Television and Radio: 250 Anecdotes*

*The Funniest People in Theater: 250 Anecdotes*

*The Funniest People Who Live Life: 250 Anecdotes*

*The Funniest People Who Live Life, Volume 2: 250 Anecdotes*

*The Kindest People Who Do Good Deeds, Volume 1: 250 Anecdotes*

*The Kindest People Who Do Good Deeds, Volume 2: 250 Anecdotes*

*Maximum Cool: 250 Anecdotes*

*The Most Interesting People in Movies: 250 Anecdotes*

*The Most Interesting People in Politics and History: 250 Anecdotes*

*The Most Interesting People in Politics and History, Volume 2: 250 Anecdotes*

*The Most Interesting People in Politics and History, Volume 3: 250 Anecdotes*

*The Most Interesting People in Religion: 250 Anecdotes*

*The Most Interesting People in Sports: 250 Anecdotes*

*The Most Interesting People Who Live Life: 250 Anecdotes*

*The Most Interesting People Who Live Life, Volume 2: 250 Anecdotes*

*Reality is Fabulous: 250 Anecdotes and Stories*

*Resist Psychic Death: 250 Anecdotes*

*Seize the Day: 250 Anecdotes and Stories*